PARENT YOURSELF AGAIN

Love Yourself the Way

You Have Always Wanted to Be Loved

Yong Kang Chan
www.nerdycreator.com

Printed in the United States of America

First Edition, 2018

ISBN 978-981-11-8159-7

Cover illustrated by Rusty Doodle
Author photo by Benson Ang
Book edited by Jessica Bryan

Your Free Gifts

FREE
SELF-LOVE GIFTS

nerdycreator.com/self-love-gifts

Low self-esteem can cause problems in your work, relationship, and mental health. After my episode of depression, I realize the importance of loving myself. So I've put together these three free gifts for you.

1. Self-Love Quiz
Do you love yourself unconditionally? Or are you too hard on yourself? I had created this quiz to help you find out how much you love yourself.

2. The Round Moon

Being an introvert, I found it challenging to fit in sometimes. This short story was written to encourage us to embrace our differences and accept ourselves.

3. Self-Love Project

This project is a compilation of 44 self-love articles I had written over a year. It includes topics such as:

- forgiving yourself
- setting boundaries
- overcoming negative self-criticism
- letting go of expectations
- being authentic, and more.

If you would like to receive any of the gifts for free, please download them at www.nerdycreator.com/self-love-gifts.

CONTENTS

Part 3: Healing the Inner Child

Preface

Ram Dass, the spiritual teacher, once said: "If you think you are so enlightened, go and spend a week with your parents." The same is true for self-compassion. If you want to know whether you love yourself or not, go and live with your parents. Not just visit them, live with them. For most of us, our conflicts and unhappiness begin with our family. Learn how to love your family and you will know how to love yourself. The opposite is true, too.

But staying with your parents is not easy. No matter how old you are, whenever you are with them, you automatically become a kid again and your parents will play their roles. If you have a difficult relationship with your parents, being around them will bring up unhappy and painful memories from the past. They will likely treat you the way they have always treated you. Were you criticized as a child? Most likely, they will continue to criticize you for the same things. Do you have narcissistic parents? They are unlikely to change much.

The relationship with our parents will not change until we change.

In this book, *Parent Yourself Again*, I encourage you to initiate change. It doesn't matter who is right or who is wrong. Be a loving presence for yourself instead of waiting for your parents or anyone else to provide you with the love and approval you seek. When we accept that our parents will never be the way we want them to be, we can stop seeking love and acceptance from them and our hearts will become lighter. Whether we are loved or not will not depend on our parents anymore. Loving ourselves becomes our responsibility, and this is something that all of us can do because we are the source of love.

Unlike the Western countries, people in Asia usually live with their parents until they get married and start their own families. So being Asian, I'm grateful that I have had many opportunities to resolve conflicts with my parents. My relationship with them has come a long way. I used to believe they didn't love me. But after clearing my misunderstanding and living with them for so many years,

I have a newfound appreciation of their love for me and have found a way to connect with them. They might not give me the type of love that I'm seeking, but I thank them for loving me in their special way.

As with my other books, most of the insights here are drawn from my own experiences and observations. If you are looking for something technical, complex, or extensively researched, this book might not be suitable for you. But if you want to learn more about self-exploration and reflection, this book will be of great value to you.

One of the biggest obstacles to self-compassion is our relationship with our parents. I hope this book provides you with the ability to resolve your childhood conflicts and live in peace with your family and others.

With much love,
Yong Kang Chan
Singapore, 2018

Running Away from My Parents

"I started running away when I was five years old. It wasn't until I was an adult that I realized what I really wanted was somebody to come after me when I was running away."

— WILLIE AAMES

There was a period of time when living at home was unbearable. I wanted to leave the house and find a place where I could avoid my parents, even if it meant that I had to rent a room and live with strangers.

However, I soon realized that this created unnecessary stress. I had to make money quickly so I could afford a place to live, but money wasn't coming in fast enough and I ended up making some rash career decisions along the way. It also made what I love to do less enjoyable.

My parents are not "bad" parents. I just wanted them to be a little more understanding and supportive, and a little less critical and controlling. I hoped they would accept me for who I am and give me the freedom to be myself, especially when it came to my career choice.

Leaving my job as an accountant in Singapore to pursue an animation career in Malaysia left a dent in our relationship, especially my relationship with my dad. Even now, he doesn't understand why I gave up a proper, stable job in accounting to pursue a "hobby" like animation. When the animation job didn't turn out to be what I had imagined, returning home was tough and humiliating. In the back of my mind, I constantly heard my parents repeating: *We told you so.*

Even when I started working as a tutor and writing in the morning, my parents would still tell me from time to time:

- You don't know how to think about the future.
- Writing doesn't even make you any money.
- You could have become a manager and owned a house by now if you had stayed in your job.
- There is no CPF (Central Provident Fund i.e. retirement fund) for people who are self-employed.

- Your aunt feels sad that you are not working anymore.

I didn't want to be angry with my parents but listening to these comments hurt greatly. I didn't want them to think there was something wrong with me — like why can't I be like everyone else, or why am I still living at home and not working. Sometimes, even when the comments were not directed at me, I would feel irritated. My elder brother also works from home as an illustrator. Every time I heard my parents talking negatively about what he did or they blamed him for influencing me to leave my job, a part of me was screaming inside: *He didn't influence me to be an author. I made my own decision!*

Why can't they let me be myself?

Why don't they understand?

Why don't they support and approve of my career choice?

The more I thought about it, the more I didn't want to be around them.

When we were children, we believed that when we grew up we would have the power and freedom to make our own choices and do whatever we wanted. But now, as adults, how many of us are still letting our parents' opinions influence our decisions and affect how we feel? How many of us are still playing the child role in relation to them?

You can leave your parents but it will not resolve your problems.

I thought that by avoiding my parents and being far away from them, I could have my freedom and be able to live a peaceful life. But I was wrong. When I was in Malaysia working as an animator for six months, I realized that no matter how far away I was, part of me yearned for their approval as though I was still five years old. Part of me resented them for not being supportive. I wanted them to love me the way I wanted them to love me. I wanted them to be supportive, understanding, and empathetic.

However, I finally realized that this fantasy of mine was never going to happen, and thinking that it would *not* happen kept me from getting stuck in an eternal loop of longing and disappointment. I began to understand that I could not depend on them to provide me with affirmation and approval. To improve my relationship with my parents, I needed to change. I needed to give myself permission and approval to do what I wanted to do. If my parents couldn't love me the way I wanted them to love me, then I would have to learn how to love myself.

When I became a "real" adult and stopped seeking approval from my parents, I let go of my unrealistic expectations of what they could do for me. I no longer tried to force them to accept my career path and I didn't have to explain anymore why I'm writing books and teaching students. I just do what makes me happy. Seeing that I'm firm in my career choice, and knowing that they can't do anything to alter my decision, they don't feel the urge to talk about my career and try to persuade me anymore.

When I accepted that my parents were unable to approve of my career choice, my relationship with them became harmonious. Previously, when I resisted their non-acceptance, I created my own suffering. Now that I have resolved my side of the issue, I am happy to stay with my parents and I no longer have the desire to run away from them.

About This Book

When I was seventeen years old, I read my first self-help book. I don't remember the title, but I still remember one of the exercises included in the book. First, imagine that your younger self is sitting in front of you and he or she has a problem. You are supposed to encourage and give this younger self advice based on the experience you have accumulated over the years. When you are one step removed from your younger self, it's easier for your younger self to share its fears and desires, and come up with solutions. This exercise can help you resolve some of the issues that you have been holding on to since you were a child.

Parent Yourself Again shares some of the same ideas. However, instead of just focusing on the younger self, we will focus on two aspects of the mind: the *inner child* and the *inner parent*. In this book, we will explore how to reconcile them so they can work together as a team. This concept is somewhat similar to the *Internal Family Systems (IFS)* therapy, which has three main parts: exiles, managers, and firefighters. However, I'm not a trained therapist and will not be using the IFS framework here. You can read more about IFS if you are interested: *Self-Therapy: A Step-By-Step Guide to Creating Wholeness and Healing Your Inner Child Using IFS, A New, Cutting-Edge Psychotherapy* by Jay Earley.

The information I share in this book is based on what I know intuitively and use for myself. You can adapt it in whatever way fits your situation. Most importantly, this book brings in *mindfulness*. Without the practice of mindfulness and the realization that we are *not* our mind, we can become carried away with our emotions and become trapped in memories from the past. For me, mindfulness simply means focusing on the present moment and being aware of and paying attention to my thoughts, emotions, and bodily sensations. Mindfulness can be practiced anywhere, even when eating a meal. Becoming mindful is a mental state that anyone can achieve with practice.

Mindfulness can also be considered a form of meditation but without the formalities of sitting on a cushion with your legs crossed and repeating a specific mantra, although I do sit down every morning to meditate in a more formal manner.

This book is suitable for anyone who had a traumatic or unfulfilling childhood. If you have an unresolved desire to be loved by your parents, or you feel numb toward them, this book can help you find peace within yourself.

You can learn to be your own loving and supportive parent.

It doesn't matter whether your parents are dead or

alive. If there is anything they failed to do for you in the past, you can learn to do it for yourself.

In the first part of the book, you will come to understand that the parent-child relationship is not just external. It also includes the relationship between the inner child and the inner parent. We will also discuss how these two aspects of ourselves are not in balance and how this can impact us. In the second part of the book, we will work on the inner parent, helping it to grow and become a better parent for our inner child. Lastly, we will help the inner child uncover and heal its deep-seated, emotional pain.

Again, as I'm a tutor, I share a lot of insights from my interactions with students and parents. So I've changed the names of the people mentioned in this book to protect their privacy.

Now, let's start by understanding the complex relationship between parents and children, and how this relationship continues to live in our minds.

PART 1

Understanding the Parent-Child Relationship

Chapter 1

There Is a Child Self and a Parent Self Within You

"For in every adult there dwells the child that was, and in every child there lies the adult that will be."

— JOHN CONNOLLY, THE BOOK OF LOST

Often times, when my gut sends me vital information, I shut it off. At the end of 2017, I returned to my previous company to cover a job for a colleague while she was away for medical reasons, but I had mixed feelings about it.

Initially, I wanted to reject their offer. My gut was screaming "no" as my manager explained the scope of the job to me over the phone. I never truly enjoy doing accounts and I felt unmotivated at the thought of doing that kind of work *again*. Most importantly, I knew that going back would disrupt the peace I had built with my parents thus far. I had been self-employed as a private tutor for two years and for the last few months my parents had finally stopped talking about my career path. Taking this part-time job in my former field would only remind them that I'm not working full-time in a stable job and not earning as much as *they think* I should. Would my parents nag at me again? No, thank you!

However, after some persuasion from the company's financial controller, I gave in. Also, there was another part of me that wanted to say "yes." I had been working under capacity for the whole year and the extra income would help pay some of the costs for my future books. Not only that, I have a good relationship with my previous colleagues, so I felt obliged to help them out of goodwill. I also felt that anyone who is sick deserves to take a break and rest. They should have peace of mind while they are on leave from a job. Even so, sometimes my empathy for others and my inability to say no gets me into trouble, such as when I agree to things that I later come to regret.

Just as I predicted, in less than two weeks of returning to my former position, my parents brought up the topic of my career path again. At first, I was rather annoyed with my dad because he kept rushing me to work even though I wasn't late. In addition to writing, one of the reasons I requested working in the afternoon was because I didn't want my dad to take me to work in the morning. I thought that if he didn't drive me to work, he wouldn't have the opportunity to rush me. Apparently, I was wrong.. His supervisory instinct is so strong that he felt the need to tell me to leave home early, even though he had no idea what my reporting time was. Fortunately, the nagging stopped when I emphasized that I was on time; I was feeling *really* stressed at work, and his constant reminders were not helping.

After the duties were handed over to me and my colleague had left for her medical break, I started to feel the pressure. Most days, including the weekends, the first thing that I woke up to was the thought of whatever deadline I was supposed to meet. Although I was only working four hours a day, the job occupied my entire mental space throughout the day. I couldn't stop thinking of the tasks I needed to do next and how to do them. It was so bad that during lunch one day my hands began to tremble involuntarily.

It was hard to focus on my job because of the anxiety I was experiencing. What's worse was that my mind couldn't stop complaining while I was working. Whenever there were more tasks to do, my mind would make a fuss over it:

This job sucks. You shouldn't have agreed to come back and cover the duties. The money is not worth your time and effort. You could have stayed at home and worked on your next book. Fortunately, I was able to quickly calm my mind down with mindfulness practices, even though I definitely felt a constant surge of anger and resentment arising within me.

Our relationship with our parents continues to live within us.

One morning during my daily meditation routine, I started to tear up. It wasn't because of stress. It wasn't self-pity, either. It was the realization that I often ignore the little voice inside me that is dying to be heard, the same voice I often heard when I was a child.

Growing up, I frequently felt neglected by my family and my peers. Being soft-spoken and with my head in the clouds, sometimes people didn't hear me, or they didn't understand what I had to say. It was also hard for me to get the attention of other people because everyone else was louder and more vocal than I was.

There was a period of time, especially in secondary school, when I had trouble making friends and getting along with my classmates. I told my dad that I wanted to change schools. But instead of hearing my reasons, he told me that my older brother was doing well in the same school and he questioned why I couldn't do the same. At the time, I wanted my dad to express more empathy, but he didn't, and I realized I had to suck it up and deal with my problems on my own.

I also developed the habit of pleasing others, in much the same way my mother does. Many times, it was at the expense of my own needs. To avoid conflict, I often found myself saying "yes" to things that I really had no intention of saying "yes" to. It reminded me of the time when I was eleven years old and I noticed that my class monitor was cheating on a test. I felt he was being unfair to the other students, so I wrote a letter about it and planned to give it to my teacher. But when I told my mom what I was going to do, she told me not to stir up trouble and ruin the relationship I had with the class monitor. As a child, I was taught to empathize with others, but also to be accommodating and not create conflict. But sadly, this meant I also grew up believing that the needs of other people were more important than mine. Now, as an adult, I find it hard to assert myself and get my own needs met.

During that meditation session, for the first time, I could *see* and *empathize* with my inner child. I had been ignoring its existence and not paying attention to what it had to say. When my gut screamed "no," I could have spent some time to acknowledge how it felt and examine why. Instead, I often agree with others without considering my deeper feelings. Whenever I get into trouble, I always tell myself that I will not do the same thing again. But time and time again, I make the same mistake of not listening to the messages my inner child sends me.

I learned that even though I have a very different personality from my parents, the way I treat my inner child is no different than how my parents treated me. I have unconsciously adopted some beliefs and habits from my parents. It's as though they continue to live within me.

The Inner Child and the Inner Parent

In my fourth book, *The Disbelief Habit*, I wrote about the various voices in each person's head. These are referred to as *subpersonalities* in psychology. The mind subdivides itself into different parts, and each part has its own unique purpose, which is intended to help us cope with different situations. In that book, I focused on the critical voice known as the *inner critic*. In this book, I'm going to introduce two other subpersonalities: the inner child, and the inner parent.

Before we begin, please bear in mind that you can call these two subpersonalities any name you want. In fact, I call my inner child, *My Little Boy*. The names given to the subpersonalities in this book are arbitrary. The mind is complex, and there's no need to define all the subpersonalities your mind has created. It's also impossible to do because sometimes there isn't a clear distinction between the various parts. Some subpersonalities might overlap others. For example, your inner critic can also be referred to as the "inner parent," if that's how you treat your inner child. I choose the word "parent" because it's neutral, something that everyone can relate to, and it does not describe a certain type of parent.

In essence, all of the subpersonalities are just part of the mind. Labeling the different parts is for illustration purposes only; in order to show you how the mind works and help you become more aware of its influence on your actions and behaviors.

The Inner Child

Many people are aware of their inner critic, but they are not as aware of their inner child. If you have an inner critic that can't stop criticizing you, and you feel hurt by it, what part of you is being criticized and feeling the pain? This subpersonality is the inner child.

Our inner child stores our memories and emotional pain, just as a child would.

Most of us can only recall important events in our childhood. The inner child tends to be pushed aside when we grow up and develop our identity as an adult. However, the unresolved hurtful feelings that we have carried since childhood still reside in our memories and body, whether we are aware of them or not.

Think of a recent time when someone said something about you that triggered an emotional reaction. Either you felt upset or angry about it, or you experienced some uncomfortable bodily sensation as a result of what they said. Ask yourself: *Why am I so convinced that they are right?* If rationally you know that the other person is wrong, why do you have a reaction to it? This is because a part of you (the inner child) is convinced that the other person is right. Our minds formed beliefs about ourselves when we were young, and as adults, we hold onto these hurtful feelings.

As an adult, you might know that the criticism isn't true. But from your inner child's perspective, it still believes they are true. Ask yourself: *How did it feel as a kid when your closest family members called you lazy, stupid, or worthless? How did it feel when your parents were busy with their work and didn't give you the attention you desired?*

When we were children, we didn't understand why our parents treated us the way they did, and we took on the blame. If there wasn't anyone to help us with our emotions, we couldn't learn how to manage or deal with our shame, anger, and fear. So we carried these unresolved emotions into adulthood, forgetting that we were once hurt as children.

If you have difficulty in becoming aware of your inner child right now, it's okay. You will get better at it as you read this book.

The Inner Parent

Thich Nhat Hanh, a Zen Buddhist monk, once said, "If you look deeply into the palm of your hand, you will see your parents and all generations of your ancestors. All of them are alive in this moment. Each is present in your body. You are the continuation of each of these people."

The inner parent is a subpersonality that resembles our parents. You might have realized that a lot of your self-talk, whether it's praise or criticism, is just a replay from your father or mother, or both. Your inner child carries wounds from your childhood, and your inner parent stores rules about what you are supposed or not supposed to do. Its function is to protect and nurture your inner child. Even if you are not a parent in real life, you will still have an inner parent. From a young age, we learned from our parents how to protect ourselves from danger and harm, how to manage ourselves and navigate the world, and what people and situations are good or bad for our growth and development, be it directly or indirectly.

Our parents are role models.
We learn how to be parents from them.

If you have parents who love themselves and are there to help you navigate childhood challenges, you have most likely learned how to take care of yourself. However, if you have parents who don't love themselves or were not there when you faced tough challenges, you might not know how to protect yourself when you grow up, because there was no one to model positive behavior for you.

This is commonly seen in abusive families. Typically, one of the parents was abusive and the other parent didn't do anything to stop the abuse. In psychology, this parent is called an "enabler." He or she enables the abusive parent to continue being abusive by not stopping it. Who do the children who grow up in these environments learn to protect themselves from? The abuser? The person who asserts his or her anger against another person? Or do they learn from the enabler, the person who keeps allowing the abuse to happen?

When our parents are people pleasers and they are unable to satisfy their own needs, we learn to disregard our needs, too. We are not taught to stand up for our rights and ask for help when we need it.

We look up to our parents for guidance, but sometimes what they teach us is not beneficial, but rather only rules and rituals passed down by our ancestors through the generations. For example, when parents tell their children not to cry and not feel angry, they are not acknowledging the children's feelings and teaching them how to manage their emotions. Many of us learn to protect ourselves by suppressing or denying our emotions and our inner child. But this only results in more conflict between the inner child and the inner parent. It can also result in health problems.

Reconciliation of the Two Subpersonalities

To reconcile the inner child and inner parent is not so much about changing the inner child to fit the inner parent's rules and beliefs. This is something that most of us are already good at doing.

Most of us have an inner parent that doesn't take care of the inner child's needs properly. They are more focused on the needs of the ego, such as pleasing other people in order to feel needed, or achieving success and getting recognition from others. This makes the inner parent happy for a short period of time, but it doesn't last. There is always a feeling of not being fulfilled, no matter how much you achieve, because the inner child's needs are not being met.

The relationship between parents and their children is complex. Some of us might feel a little resentful toward our parents. We might be frustrated with them for being so controlling and critical. But yet, we feel a little guilty for having these feelings because our parents raised us and we love them. Having mixed feelings about your parents is quite normal. If your parents have always ignored your needs, resentment is bound to occur.

The same applies to the relationship between your

inner child and inner parent. For those of us who have problems asserting the needs of our inner child, we end up directing this resentment toward our inner parent, which results in self-blame. The inner child feels angry and stressed that it is forced to do something it doesn't want to do or believes it can't. It blames the inner parent for disregarding its emotions and giving in to other people's needs and societal wants.

In my case, my inner child definitely doesn't want to do accounting again. "He" doesn't like to do tasks with such tight deadlines because it is stressful to deal with a large amount of information in a short period of time. But my inner parent just went ahead and agreed on the engagement without even consulting the inner child. The result of this hasty decision was inner conflict. The inner child kept complaining and interrupting my work. "He" believed that "he" could not manage the deadlines, while the inner parent believed that "he" could.

However, I'm not saying that the inner child is always right and you have to do what it demands.

Neither subpersonality is correct.

The inner child can be reckless with its desires, too, but

you have to acknowledge its feelings. You have to listen to both sides before coming to a decision. Both your inner child and inner parent need to be heard before you can live in peace. To maintain inner peace, it's important to reconcile these two different perspectives. You can't force or push either of them aside. Otherwise, one of them will be unhappy. This is what your true self, the spiritual self, the source of love, is here to do — observe both sides and be the neutral party. I would probably still pick up the part-time job at my ex-company, but I would have at least stopped and listened to my inner child's point of view and understand how "he" feels.

It's not enough to just heal the inner child. Our inner parent has to change, too. It needs to learn how to properly protect and nurture the inner child and take care of the inner child's needs. When our inner parent fails to perform its responsibilities, our inner child will continue to be exposed to events that trigger hurt feelings, and we will end up acting unconsciously because of these feelings, just like a child.

Chapter 2

How Your Childhood Affects Your Adult Life

"Parents are the ultimate role models for children. Every word, movement and action has an effect. No other person or outside force has a greater influence on a child than the parent."

— BOB KEESHAN

I'm a fan of the reality TV show, *Survivor*, but there is one episode in *Survivor 30: Worlds Apart* that was so painful to watch that I almost didn't want to watch the rest of the season.

During the Survivor Auction, Will Sims II spent $100 to buy a covered item, only to find out that he had bought himself out of the auction and he was being sent back to camp immediately. Upon arrival at the camp, though, he found a clue that led him to uncover a hidden box with rations in it. He was given the option to share this information with his other tribe members or keep it to himself, and he decided to share the food with everyone.

However, suspecting there was more food than what Will had shared, Shirin Oskooi and the two other castaways started spreading rumors that Will might have hidden some food for himself. Later, when Will found out from someone else that they were questioning his integrity, he got really angry. He started lashing out at Shirin, who was the only one of the three castaways in the camp at the time.

Things got brutal when Will took it too far and made some personal attacks on Shirin, "Nobody likes you. I can guarantee that nobody at home in the United States right now is missing you. We all have loved ones who care for us, but you have nothing. You have no family. You have no soul."

It was hard to watch this confrontation. No one deserves to be verbally attacked like that. Plus, Shirin just sat there and allowed herself to be attacked. She could have just walked away when things became heated, but she sat there until her ally, Mike Holloway, came back to camp and took her away. Later, in the tribal council, Shirin revealed that her family had been ripped apart because of domestic violence. Before beating her up, her dad used to speak exactly like Will had. She had no one to save her.

Watching this episode, it's easy to empathize with Shirin. But at the same time, she no longer was the kid who was abused by her dad. She was no longer helpless and she had the power to walk away. Why did she freeze as though she was still the same abused child she once was? Why didn't she protect herself?

We often behave like we are still children.

And it's not just Shirin. I was like that, too. About half a year after this particular episode was aired, I found myself in a similar situation. As depicted in my memoir, *The Emotional Gift*, I met a random person who belittled me and let me know how bad I am. Even though he didn't verbally assault me like Will did Shirin, I just sat there and allowed the conversation to continue. I didn't even defend myself or walk away. I froze. It was only when I went back home and thought about this incident that I felt disgusted.

Finally, I realized why it was so painful to watch the scene between Will and Shirin. Watching it, I felt like it was me who was sitting there. And, just like Shirin, I was being lashed out by Will and was not able to do anything about it.

I was reminded of all the times when I didn't love myself enough to stand up against or walk away from the hurtful comments of others.

As disturbing this episode was, it made both Shirin and I realize that our childhood wounds still hurt us and affect our actions. Even though we have become adults, we still behave like children sometimes, if not most of the time. All of us have habits and beliefs that we have learned and developed since childhood, and we still rely heavily on them.

However, not all of us are aware of it. Some of us have already forgotten our unpleasant childhood memories, or we think we have outgrown them. We believe we have total control over our behavior, but we don't realize that a lot of our actions are still unconsciously dictated by our childhood experiences and trauma. Our inner child remembers and stores the pain. However, the pain is merely suppressed by our inner parent to protect us from feeling hurt.

In this chapter, we will widen our awareness as we uncover four of the common effects our childhood can have on us.

Your Standards Remain the Same

If you compare your current standards with the ones you had as a child, how much has changed? Are you still using the same standards?

People who had abusive, critical, and/or controlling parents often find themselves caught in similar situations with others. When we were children, we were too weak to protect ourselves from harm. Our parents determined our lives and made decisions on our behalf. There was nothing much we could do as children except try to find a way of coping with the situation.

Even though coping helped us survive childhood, some of us have unconsciously accepted these behaviors as normal. We find it difficult to quit unhealthy relationships because we are so used to coping with them that we have developed a bigger capacity to accept the wrongdoings of others. We might not even know there's anything wrong with our relationships until they get worse. Unlike people who don't have such negative childhood experiences, we are more likely to settle for undesirable relationships and stay in them longer than we should.

Our inner parent didn't grow.

We have grown taller and bigger. As adults, we are capable of protecting ourselves from harm, but that doesn't mean our interior has changed. Our inner parent still uses the same standards it adopted many years ago to guide the inner child. Most of us have not updated this internal standard, so we relate to others the same way we once related to our parents, and we allow our inner child to get hurt repeatedly.

In my case, I'm so used to keeping the peace and not arguing with my dad (which is just what my mom used to do) that I automatically become submissive when someone criticizes me. It has never occurred to me that I can assert my own opinion, defend myself, or walk away when someone puts me down. My inner parent just sits there and allows someone to tear my inner child apart as though nothing is happening. This is the standard behavior my inner parent has adopted. Not only does this behavior affect my relationship with my parents, it also affects the relationships I have with everyone else.

Do you take care of your own needs well? Do you find it easy to give but hard to receive? If you have a constant desire to please others and seek their approval, check and see if one or both of your parents also have such tendencies. You might have copied your standards of behavior from them.

Your Parents Influence Your Choices

Have you ever wondered why alcoholics often have alcoholic parents? Or why adults who are neglected as children are often attracted to narcissistic partners?

As adults, we know that some choices are bad for us, but we still make them. A child who has a parent who exhibits compulsive behaviors, such as alcohol abuse, gambling, or overeating, tends to adopt the same habits as their parents when they become adults. Children look to their parents for guidance and follow how their parents cope with challenges and emotions. If they are not exposed to healthy ways of coping with difficult feelings such as stress and anger during childhood, they are likely to use the same coping mechanisms as their parents.

Our childhood experiences also affect our choice of a partner. We tend to seek partners that are similar to our parents. Part of this is due to familiarity. The other reason is that we project the image of our parents onto our partners. For example, children who feel neglected by their parents often seek partners who are cold and aloof, even though there are so many other potential partners who are warm and giving. We want to get our emotional needs met, but we end up choosing someone who doesn't readily give us the attention we desire, just like our parents. We have an unconscious desire to get our partner to change and love us the way we want to be loved in order to satisfy the unmet needs and fantasies of our inner child. As children, we always dreamed about how nice it would be if our neglectful parents would pay some attention to us. When we grow up, we project this fantasy onto our partners.

The more you don't want to be like your parents, the more you will resemble them.

Some of us swore that we would never be like our parents. We want to be the total opposite of them. But our decision is still influenced by their actions and non-action. So in essence, we are still using the behaviors of our parents as a starting point in building our values.

In my case, I didn't want to be as materialistic as my dad, nor did I want to be careless with the way I spent money like my mom. So growing up, I wanted to go for my passion instead of money, and yet be extremely careful with my money. But in the end, the less I cared about making money, the more worried I was about having no money. Also, I realized that even though I was saving on little purchases, I tended to make impulsive, big purchases and waste a lot of money on unnecessary things. Ironic, isn't it? The more you don't want something in your life, the more you are controlled by it.

When you hate your parents or dislike certain traits that they have, you are actually giving them more attention and directing your energy toward them. They occupy your headspace, so how could it not affect your choices in life.

Self-Sabotage

Shane is one of my students and he has no motivation to study. After talking with him for a few weeks, I realized he has an inner conflict. Part of him (the inner parent) wants to study and follow his parents' wishes, but there is also a part of him (the inner child) that wants to rebel and not do well on his examinations. His inner conflict resembles the conflict he has with his parents.

Shane is an active child and he has ADHD. He has a flair for sports, especially basketball. But his mom wants him to study hard and work in an office. Shane has no motivation to study because getting good grades means that he will end up in administrative office work, something he doesn't want. This isn't the first time he has felt this way. Previously, he didn't do too well in his primary school examinations, but his parents forced him to get into a better program even though his score barely qualified him for the better program. Shane told me that he regrets doing so well on his exams. He said that if he had gotten one or two marks lower, he wouldn't have to face so much pressure now.

In his mind, he has all the reasons necessary to sabotage himself. If he fails his examination, his parents will not be able to force him to work in the office and he will get to do what he wants. Hence, he chooses to not pay attention in class and makes no effort to study.

You might think it's silly for Shane to think this way. But he wasn't aware that a part of him was sabotaging his effort until we talked about it. He just thought he was lazy and had no interest in studying.

Most of us are unaware of our self-sabotage.

Just like our parents, our inner parent knows or thinks it knows what is good for us, but often the inner child sabotages our efforts secretly when its needs are not met or acknowledged, and its pain and suffering are not dealt with. Knowing that the inner parent will not approve of their actions, the inner child acts discreetly through our subconscious without being caught by the inner parent. This is exactly how young children evade punishment when getting their desires met. They do it when the parents are not noticing.

Once in a while, we might experience an unusual outburst of anger, and we are shocked by it. We love someone and we know the person loves us, but somehow we feel that we can't commit to the relationship or trust the person. We procrastinate and resist doing whatever is expected of us, but we don't understand why we feel so unmotivated. Even a simple task that we know we are capable of completing can cause us to feel unreasonably anxious and fearful.

If this is happening in your life, you might want to examine whether your inner child is secretly working in the background to sabotage your efforts. It doesn't need to be in the seat of your consciousness to get what it wants.

Self-Perception

In my third book, *Empty Your Cup*, I explained that our parents are usually the first people from whom we derive our sense of self. Many of us grew up adopting our parents' views without realizing that these are their views, not necessarily ours. I teach young children mathematics, and whenever I hear them say something negative about themselves, I know that their parents or somebody close to them must have said the exact same thing to them.

For example, once I taught a girl who always used laziness as an excuse to avoid doing her work. True enough, when I talked to her mom, the first thing her mom said was that her daughter was very lazy and needed the extra lessons to gain discipline. At the back of my mind, I was wondering: *Is the student lazy because she is just naturally lazy? Or is the student lazy because her mom has told her she is lazy so many times that she now believes she is lazy?* The mom is actually a loving and compassionate person. But when she uses such labels on her child to explain her daughter's disobedience, she unwittingly encourages her daughter to be lazy.

Of course, not all children cope with criticism in the same way. The psychological effect of criticism on children depends on how they react. Some children choose to fight back or blame others for their problems instead of feeling unworthy. Mostly, it depends on our interpretation of the situation. But it's undeniable that the way our parents view us can affect our self-perception to a certain extent. When you were a child and your parents kept repeating the same things to you— and you didn't have someone to check their opinions against —it is quite likely that you will accept your parents' point of view.

The inner child stores and accumulates negative self-beliefs, which are then used as reasons to support self-sabotage.

- *Why did I lose my temper again? I'm weak. I need to show them I'm strong and not a pushover.*
- *Why can't I trust my potential mate? No one will love me when they get to know me.*
- *Why do I procrastinate? I'm a lazy person.*
- *Why do I feel anxious about doing this task? Maybe I can't do it because I'm just not good enough!*

We sabotage ourselves because we are so used to believing the false self-perceptions we have developed and believed since childhood.

Even though we are adults, our childhood still affects our standards, our choices, our actions, and our sense of self. Many of us try to change the environment and the people around us to fit our worldview. We try to change our parents and our partners in order to get the love and approval we need. But often times, it's easier and more effective to look within ourselves and mend the unhealthy parent-child relationship from within.

Chapter 3

Balance the Power Within

"We do not need magic to transform our world. We carry all the power we need inside ourselves already."

— J.K. ROWLING

"If you don't listen to me, just go ahead," said my dad, after I told him I was going to Taiwan. Then he hung up on me.

Ten years ago, after my university graduation, my friends and I were excited to go for our graduation trip to Taiwan. It would be my first trip overseas. For the past twenty-four years, I had never left Singapore, and I couldn't wait to see and experience another country and its culture. But at the same time, I was afraid to tell my dad about it. I had tested the waters at home before I booked the flights and accommodations with my friends, and he had not seemed pleased.

Until then, my parents had gone overseas on their own a couple of times, but they had never taken my brothers and me with them. My dad had an irrational fear that the whole family might die in a plane crash, and there would be no one to pass down the family line if that happened. He doesn't like to travel on a plane, himself, and he seldom traveled.

But sure, he will agree to it, won't him? I thought to myself. *I'm not traveling with the rest of my family. Furthermore, my brothers previously went overseas for army training so I'm sure he won't mind.*

After watching my friends call their parents and get permission for the trip, I gathered my courage and called my dad.

I never expected he would be so angry that he would hang up the phone on me. My heart sank when I heard his words: "If you don't listen to me, just go ahead."

I usually feel rather uncomfortable about dealing with another person's anger, especially my dad's. But later that night, I protested and asked him why my brothers were allowed to go overseas and I was not. He told me that travel was compulsory for them because they were fulfilling their obligations to the nation. In my case, the proposed travel was recreational and I didn't need to go.

His reasoning didn't make much sense. Did he mean that I couldn't travel for the rest of my life unless the government or my employer made me? Even though I'm obedient, I had already paid for the flights and accommodations and told my friends that I was coming with them. There's no way I was going to ask for a refund and disappoint them. Furthermore, I was already twenty-four years old and I should be allowed to make my own decisions.

So despite his disapproval, I knew I had to go to Taiwan.

I knew I had to disobey.

We are always children in our parents' eyes.

Finding Nemo is one of my favorite animated films of all time. Apart from the interesting characters and humor, it reminds me of my relationship with my dad. The story is about a clownfish named "Marlin," who is very protective of his son "Nemo." During the opening scene, we see why Marlin is afraid to be out in the ocean. He has lost his wife and their eggs during a barracuda attack. To him, the ocean is dangerous. Also, Nemo has a broken fin and can't swim very well. So he constantly warns his son about the danger of the ocean. On the first day of school, being angry at his father's controlling ways, Nemo swam out in the ocean to touch the boat just to spite his father. He was then caught by a scuba diver and sent to a dentist office far away from home. The rest of the movie depicts Marlin's journey to find his son.

I can relate to Nemo because I also have a "broken fin" and an overprotective dad. When I was eight, I had epilepsy. My dad had to carry me to the hospital and he slept on a foldable bed next to me. I knew how worried my parents were at the time. But I was fine after a couple of seizures and medicine, and I grew up to be a healthy kid. However, in my parents' eyes, I will always be a weak, little child who needs their protection.

When I disobeyed my dad and went to Taiwan, I didn't do it out of spite. Both of us had something to learn. I had to learn how to assert myself, and he had to learn how to let go of control. He can't control my brothers and me forever, especially now that we are adults.

Ever since I made the first move and opened the floodgate, my dad has been less concerned about us traveling abroad. We have more freedom to travel with our friends and even alone. However, we still haven't traveled together as a family.

The Power Imbalance

No matter how loving your parents are toward you, there will always be an imbalance in power, unlike in other relationships such as friendships and intimate relationships where both parties can have an equal standing. The moment you are born, your parents are in a more superior position than you. You might have the best parents in the world, but you are still dependent. You must listen to and follow your parents for survival. Even if they don't assert their superiority, you will continue to see them as authority figures and ask them for permission in almost every aspect of your life.

Most parents assert their superiority over their children whether it's intentional or not, especially when it comes to knowledge. Most parents believe they have more experience and knowledge than their children. They think they know what's good or bad for their kids, so their kids have to listen to them. Yes, parents have the responsibility to guide, nurture, and protect their kids. But when an adult is teaching or disciplining someone, it's easy to slip into the "I know more than you" mode and not consider or consult the other person's point of view and feelings.

All children feel powerless to a certain degree.

Sometimes, my students tell me that it's pointless to talk to their parents because they are never going to listen. When we were children, we didn't get many opportunities to express our viewpoints and feelings, and sometimes when we did, we were ignored. Our parents couldn't provide us with everything we desired and we had no power to get what we desired on our own. Other than pleading with our parents and winning their favor, there's nothing much we could have done. Many of us felt so powerless during childhood that we eventually gave up trying.

Furthermore, if you have parents who believe they are always right— and who are over-identified with their role of being a parent and the power they have over their children — you might feel even more powerless and subjugated. When your parents tell you what to do all the time, you don't have much freedom to do what you truly desire. If you disobey them, they might feel angry or sad and this makes you feel afraid or guilty. Your growth is stifled, especially when you become a teen and start to develop your own identity.

I have a friend, Zane, who used to be left-handed. But

since childhood, he has been punished and forced to use his right hand. When he was young, he was forced to learn drawing, which he didn't enjoy. He often felt stressed and pressured to attend the extra art lessons scheduled by his parents. His mom is in the accounting industry and guess what? Now Zane is in the accounting industry, too. He doesn't enjoy his job, but he doesn't know what he wants in life. Ever since he was young, his parents have dictated everything that he does, so much so that he has lost sight of his true desires and individuality.

On the contrary, there are also parents who don't enforce much control over their kids. Some parents don't guide their children enough, and some are so helpless that the children have to take care of their parents. Even though there seems to be a role reversal here between the parent and the child, it doesn't mean the child has more power than the parent. The child is still a child. Taking care of his or her parents is just a way to get love from the parents. The same goes for children who have parents who are absent or divorced. They feel powerless to get the love and attention they want, and frustrated in their efforts to keep their parents together.

The inner child has accumulated a lot of hurt feelings and suffered greatly since childhood. Some children can't wait to grow up. They always thought that when they were adults, they would finally be able to do the things they always wanted and have control over their lives. Some thought that by being obedient, more helpful, or more successful, their parents would finally give them the approval and love they desire. Little do they know that the power imbalance between them and their parents will continue to exist and their relationships will remain the same, even when they become adults.

Why Is It Difficult to Change Your Parents?

Many of us want a good relationship with our parents. We want our relationship with them to improve and be more positive. But we often fail to achieve this goal because our parents are not as interested in improving the relationship as we are. They don't recognize the need for improvement because, unlike us, they don't believe there is a problem.

Ideally, parents should adjust their parenting style as their children grow and change. Dealing with an infant is different than dealing with a five-year-old, and relating to a teen is different than relating to a child who has become an adult. But most parents treat their adult children like they are still young. They are so used to taking care of their children's needs and dictating their actions that it has become a habit. They never give their children a chance to be adults, let alone perceive them as equals.

Most parents can't quit their role as parents.

My mom still tells us what to do sometimes, instead of asking us for help. If she wants something to be done immediately, she nags at us constantly or calls us from the other room until she gets her way. My dad is the same. It took him a long time to accept that he has lost control over us. He just can't get us to do things his way anymore.

If you have a friend who is twenty or thirty years older than you, they don't tell you what to do. They are not disappointed when you don't listen to their advice. Perhaps in some Asian countries, they might. But even if they do, you don't feel a need to obey them. They have no power over you unless they are your superiors at work.

But the relationship between our parents and us is different. We are overly identified as their children, and they are overly identified as our parents. We have grown from being dependent to independent, so you would expect the adult-child relationship to evolve into an adult-adult relationship. But no, it doesn't. Our parents still want us to be dependent on them, consciously or unconsciously.

In a way, there is some pride attached to being a parent and someone who knows more than their children. Many parents find it difficult to accept that their children have grown up and are capable of making their own decisions. Acceptance could mean the loss of power, control, and the feeling of worthiness that can be derived from being needed and depended on. For parents who see their children as an extension of themselves, they might feel as though they have lost one of their possessions or control over a part of themselves that they value. It's even worse for sick and aging parents because they are forced to depend on their children and this really hurts the ego.

Most parents do not want to perceive us differently, *i.e.,* as adults, because it means they would have to change. Subconsciously, they criticize us, control our actions, or offer unsolicited opinions to keep us at a level that is familiar to them, and so they don't have to change. Those of us who react or blame our parents only feed their ego and remain controlled by them. The same goes for those of us who try to change our parents or want them to see us in a better light.

We are partly responsible for this power imbalance because we continue to play the role of a child with our parents. Some of us continue to ask for their approval, even though we get a lot of affirmations from other sources. When I was quitting my first job as an auditor, I remember how desperately I sought my parents' blessings and approval. I was so used to letting them make decisions on my behalf that I felt stuck and trapped when they didn't support my decision to quit.

We might have grown up, but our relationship with our parents hasn't changed much. Our roles still remain the same. Their perception of us remains the same as when we were young and incapable of surviving on our own. We still relate to them as though our livelihood depends on them. If you want to have a better relationship with your parents, it's easier to change yourself from within than to try and "fix" them.

Heal the Relationship Within You

The power imbalance you experience externally with your parents is also inside of you. The relationship between your inner child and your inner parent resembles your childhood relationship with your parents. Your inner parent believes that it has complete control over your inner child and it can get your inner child to do what it wants.

Your inner child feels oppressed and tries to gain some control through subtle means.

Have you ever witnessed something like this? You are shopping in a supermarket or a departmental store, and then all of a sudden there is a crying kid throwing a tantrum in public. The parent says, "If you don't come with me, I'm going to leave without you," and starts to walk away. The kid cries even louder and doesn't want to leave.

Sometimes, the kid will stop crying and follow the parent out of the store. Other times, the parents give up because they are soft-hearted, annoyed, or they feel so embarrassed in public that they forget they have control over their kids. Throwing a tantrum is a kid's way of getting what they want. They know they can't win and their parents have all the control. But by refusing to cooperate, they are able to gain some control. We experience this battle of control internally, too. Sometimes, our inner child refuses to cooperate and our inner parent has no choice but to give in.

**If you can balance the power within you,
you will also know how to relate to your parents.**

There isn't much difference between these two types of

relationships. Use the internal relationship between your subpersonalities as a practice ground to gain insights on how to relate to your parents. Even though relationships require effort from both parties, when you heal your side of the relationship, your relationship with your parents will naturally improve, too. You might find yourself being less reactive to their actions and have more compassion for them and yourself.

In the next two sections, you will discover how to create a power balance between your inner child and inner parent. First, we will bring the power level of our inner parent down so the inner child feels safe to talk about its needs, desires, and suffering. This will allow us to bring the power level of the inner child up to a level that is equal to the inner parent.

PART 2

Growing Your Inner Parent

Chapter 4

The Responsibilities of Your Inner Parent

"Parents can only give good advice or put them on the right paths, but the final forming of a person's character lies in their own hands."

— ANNE FRANK

.

Three years ago, I attended an entrepreneur program in Bali. In one of the seminars, the chef discussed health and well-being. She said that moms know best, and they sure know the best food for their children. I didn't quite agree, so I said: "Not my mom. She always buys junk food and snacks for us." The chef replied, "You could buy healthy food for your family, and then eat it instead of the junk food that your mom offers."

This was a slap in my face, but she was right. I realized

that I was being so childish. When my mom buys snacks, it doesn't mean that I have to eat them. Even if my mom offers me junk food, I can reject it. I don't have to oblige. Why do I let her dictate what I should eat and then blame her for it? As an adult, I need to take responsibility for my own health and my own life.

When you assign responsibility for your life to someone else, you are giving away your power.

Part of being an adult is to take responsibility. Children don't have to take responsibility for their actions because their parents make most of their decisions for them. If they make mistakes, it's understandable, because they are still young. Their parents should be there to guide them. But when we grow up, we are responsible for our own decisions and meeting our own needs. We don't wait for our parents to give us permission. It's not their responsibility anymore. It's ours. The shift from being a teenager to an adult is so gradual that sometimes we don't understand the responsibilities we are required to take on as adults.

Your parents might have neglected or abused you in the past. They might still be criticizing you and hurting you with their words and actions. It's tempting to blame them for your childhood misery. But, as an adult, you have to take care of yourself and take full responsibility for your actions and your life. If someone serves you poison, you can choose not to drink it. You might not have had a choice when you were a child, but no one can force you now that you are an adult.

Even though there's nothing we can do to change what happened during our childhood, we can teach our inner parent to be a better parent for our inner child. Our inner child has unfulfilled needs that are waiting to be satisfied, but we can't assign this responsibility to our birth parents and depend on them.

First, you understand what you need the most, and you are the best one who can understand your inner child's deepest desires. If your parents understood your needs when you were a child, and they knew how to satisfy those needs, they probably would have done so already. My parents are not in touch with their own emotions and, therefore, they can't help me fulfill the emotional connection that my inner child desires. Only I can. It's my job to understand the different emotions and triggers of my inner child. Who can do it for me if I can't even do that for my inner child?

Second, if you keep depending on your parents to satisfy your needs, you are not allowing your inner parent to grow. When I was working in Malaysia for six months, being separated from my parents was a good learning experience. Working overseas helped me learn how to be more responsible and take care of myself. I had to source my own food, do my laundry, pay the electric bills, and all the little things my parents did for me that I had taken for granted. When you are with your parents, you naturally play the role of the child, and your parents naturally play their roles as parents. You don't get to fully experience what is it like to be an adult and develop adult skills.

Indeed, it's the parents' responsibility to take care of their children, and some of them didn't do a good job. However, we are capable of taking care of ourselves now, and we have to take over these responsibilities from our parents. If we don't know how to be a good parent, we need to learn. We don't have to wait until we become parents of a newborn baby before we develop these skills. We can start practicing how to be a good parent by learning how to take care of our inner child.

And one of the first responsibilities of our inner parent is to understand what our inner child needs.

Understand the Needs of Your Inner Child

The Basic Needs of a Child

If you have been neglecting your inner child, it will be difficult for you to know what your inner child needs. In the chapters to come, I'll share some ways to get your inner child to open up.

But for now, let's think about the basic needs of a child. Every child has the same basic needs. If you have no idea what your inner child needs, think about your children. What do they need? This will give you a general idea of what your inner child needs. If you don't have any children, imagine what you would like to give your child when you have one. If this is difficult for you to imagine, think about what you needed as a child.

Here are some basic needs of children to get you started:

- They want to be loved and valued.
- They want to be seen and heard.
- They want to be themselves and be accepted for who they are.
- They want to feel like they belong and are

connected with others.

- They want to feel safe and secure.
- They want to have the freedom to do what they want, or at least express what they want to do.

The inner child needs all of this, too. But similar to most parents, our inner parent tends to only provide food, shelter, and clothing. Yes, these are basic survival needs that keep the child secure, and they are the easiest to recognize and fulfill. But after a certain level is reached, the inner child doesn't need any more money and success. They don't need more toys like fancy cars or bigger houses. These things don't provide more security for our inner child. Their physical and safety needs have already been met. These things only help to inflate the ego of our inner parent.

They really need their inner parents to care for and love them. According to Maslow's hierarchy of needs, after our physiological and safety needs are met, we have the desire to meet our needs for love and belonging and esteem. But how many times have we suppressed our emotions when our inner child tried to express pain? How many times have we ignored our heart's desires and chased after what society or others believe is good for us?

We think that we know what's best for our inner child. But more often than not, we don't. We model our inner parent after our birth parents, who teach us how to be parents by their example. If they knew how to love us the way we wanted to be loved, we wouldn't still felt so unloved, even though we are now adults.

The Specific Needs of Your Inner Child

Apart from meeting the basic needs of your inner child, the child also has specific needs that are unique to their childhood experiences. Understanding these specific needs will help the inner parent connect with the inner child better and know what to provide for the child. There is no perfect job description for a parent or detailed instructions to follow. You have to figure out the specific needs of your inner child on your own and customize your parenting style accordingly.

Here are a few examples to help you get started:

The Abandoned Child

This inner child is afraid to be separated from others. It constantly feels that the people it is close to might leave and abandon it. Maybe one or both of your parents left you when you were young, perhaps due to divorce or death.

Maybe they were constantly away from home for most of your childhood.

This inner child has the desire to cling to others and relationships. When one relationship ends, it quickly finds another to fill the gap. It needs the inner parent to be there and help it feel safe.

The Neglected Child

This inner child feels that there is no one there for it. It feels unimportant and that something deeply missing from its life. Perhaps your parents did not give you enough attention when you were young, or they were cold to you for their own reasons. Perhaps they were too busy with their own lives or had their own issues to deal with and they had no time to care about you and your feelings.

This inner child has been ignored since you were young, so it often feels invisible, inferior, and defective compared to others. Your inner parent needs to acknowledge the inner child's feelings and worth, and give it more attention and encouragement.

The Oppressed Child

This inner child feels that it has no say over what happens in life. It feels like it has to always be accommodating to other people's wishes. In this case, your parents did not give you the space to express your opinions and feelings when you were young. You had to do what you were told or else they would become unhappy or angry.

This inner child feels forced to do things against its wishes. When your inner child has anger that is not expressed, it will find ways to sabotage your efforts. Your inner parent needs to genuinely consider its point of view and not dismiss its opinions so quickly. This inner child needs to be heard.

The Abused Child

This inner child has a lot of mixed feelings, including fear and anger at the abuser. At the same time, it might also blame itself for the abuse, especially if the abuser is someone close to you, such as your parents.

This inner child might feel more unworthy than the others discussed here. But yet, the inner parent often suppresses these hurtful feelings. This inner child has difficulty trusting others. Your inner parent needs to encourage the inner child to express its emotions instead of numbing them. Your inner parent also needs to rebuild trust with your inner child so it feels safe to share its feelings with you.

The Anxious Child

This inner child often feels that something bad is about to happen and it doesn't trust its ability to resolve problems on its own. Growing up, your parents might not have given you enough protection to make you feel safe.

This inner child has a lot of fear and worries a lot. It's hard to get this child to do anything outside of the norm because it doesn't like changes. Instead of overprotecting your inner child from harm, your inner parent needs to soothe its anxiety and encourage it to take baby steps when change is necessary.

Two Important Functions of Your Inner Parent

Identifying your inner child's needs forms the foundation of loving your inner child. In this book, we talk about two other functions of the inner parent that are crucial. One is to protect the inner child; the other is to nurture it.

Ideally, for children to grow up healthy, they need to have both a protective and a nurturing figure in the family to model themselves after. Unfortunately, this is rarely the case. Even if there are protective and nurturing figures, one tends to overpower the other.

To most people, the protective figure refers to the

father and the nurturing figure refers to the mother. But this isn't always true. Some mothers can be more protective than fathers, and some fathers can be more nurturing than mothers. The roles are not gender-specific. It doesn't matter if you are male or female. To grow your inner parent and love your inner child, you need to learn how to be both protective and nurturing. Both roles have different responsibilities but are equally important.

We tend to favor one role more than the other. For example, one might be too protective of themselves and not nurture themselves enough. They might use harsh words and disciplinary ways to control their inner child's desires and actions, keeping it from making mistakes or achieving goals that the inner parent desires. They often don't validate their inner child's needs and emotions. Other people might love their inner child to the extent that they don't set any limits to curb their inner child's actions and indulgence.

Even though one role might be stronger, it doesn't mean that we don't have any work to do on it. Overprotection and over-nurturing can harm the inner child, too. We need to tone down the stronger function a little, while also developing the skills we are lacking.

The role of your inner parent is different from your social role.

One thing to note is not to confuse your inner parent's role with your social role. Some parents take their work roles home with them and are unable to separate their role at home from their role at work. The parent of one of my students asked me for a weekly report on her child's behavior. I had to rate the child on a scale from one to ten. Doesn't this sound very much like doing an annual appraisal in a company? My dad is a supervisor at work and also at home. He doesn't realize that we are not his subordinates and we don't enjoy being monitored by him.

You might be an empathetic and nurturing person to others, but not half as loving to yourself. When we talk about these roles, we are referring to how your inner parent treats your inner child. We are talking about the home within you. It has nothing to do with how your inner parent interacts with other people outside your home.

Below is a summary of the responsibilities for each role. In the next two chapters, we'll explore each function in greater depth.

The Protective Function

One function of the inner parent is to make sure the inner child feels safe. This could be in terms of providing guidance and structure for the inner child. It could also be about setting boundaries and maintaining them so your inner child doesn't get hurt by others. Or it could be something basic, like making sure you are financially secure and have enough food and other necessities. Anything that represents strength and allows the inner child to feel they have a strong person to depend on is part of the protective function.

When your inner parent is a pillar of strength for your inner child, it prevents the inner child from feeling anxious and going into a panic. It also gives the inner child the courage to act with regard to people and situations they are afraid of.

The Nurturing Function

The other function of the inner parent is to make sure the inner child feels loved and like they belong. This is about giving your inner child support and understanding. It's about being empathetic to your inner child and acknowledging the difficulties it is going through. Sometimes, the inner parent is also there to help soothe the intense emotions the inner child has difficulty dealing with and help it understand how to handle these emotions.

Love from the inner parent makes the inner child feel accepted, understood, seen, and heard. It makes the inner child feels important and safe to express its feelings without feeling judged.

Chapter 5

Protect the Inner Child

"I cannot think of any need in childhood as strong as the need for a father's protection."

— SIGMUND FREUD

Once, there were three children living in the same neighborhood, Adam, Betty, and Calvin. They had very different parents.

Adam's parents tended to be aggressive and overprotective. He still remembers the time his dad yanked him away from the road and started beating him non-stop, screaming, "How many times have I told you not to run near the roads? You could have gotten yourself killed! Why don't you listen? Why are you so playful? Are you an idiot?" Even though Adam understands his dad's good intention of protecting him from getting hurt, he still feels traumatized by this event.

Adam's relationship with his mom is not much better. She loves to micromanage him. Ever since Adam was young, his mom has wanted to be involved in everything he does. She checks his homework in detail, wants to know who he hangs out with in school, and assumes she can decide his career path for him. She is afraid that Adam can't handle these things on his own and that he might befriend the wrong people. She is obsessed with her son's life and confuses her need to control with love for her son.

Betty has parents who are also protective, but they are firm and gentle in their approach. When Betty makes a mistake, her parents sit down with her and try to help her understand what she could have done better. One time, Betty was running toward the road and her dad stopped her just in time. Instead of expressing his anger and his fear of losing his child, her dad squatted down and looked her in the eyes and explained in a gentle manner how dangerous it was. "Hey my dear princess, when you run toward the road so suddenly the drivers might not be able to stop their cars in time and they might knock you down. Remember yesterday when you fell down? Remember how painful it was? Being knocked down by a car is much more painful than that. You don't want to get hurt, do you? So be careful and look out for cars, okay?"

Even though Betty's mom cares about her homework, she trusts Betty enough to do it on her own. Her mom only steps in to help when she sees that Betty is having difficulties or when Betty asks her for help. She believes that making mistakes is part of the learning process and she encourages Betty to make mistakes so she can learn from them. Betty feels that she has the freedom to choose what she wants to do, but at the same time she is given enough guidance to help her make sensible decisions.

Calvin's parents are free-spirited and easy-going. They don't spend much time teaching their son or establish any limits. They believe their son should be given the freedom to be himself and do whatever he loves to do. However, Calvin wishes his parents would care more about him and give him some guidance. He has had many bruises and scars because his parents let him run freely around the house and jump from furniture to furniture. When he was a teenager, a car nearly knocked him down because he was so focused on retrieving a soccer ball that had flown onto the road. Luckily, the car stopped just in time. As a child, he was never told to be careful of the road, so he didn't learn how to look out for cars.

To other kids, Calvin seems blessed. His parents allow him to watch TV until late at night. When he did badly on his examinations, his parents didn't scold him, so Calvin didn't pay much attention to his studies and as a result, he didn't get into the course he wanted. Although Calvin is given a lot of freedom, he ends up living recklessly because he is not given enough guidance and structure.

What about you?

How does your inner parent protect your inner child?

Are you overprotective of your inner child, or not protective enough?

Is your inner parent overprotective like an inner critic, constantly judging what you do and controlling your actions? Or does it allow your inner child to run wild and dictate what you do?

Sometimes, it can be both. We swing between these two extremes from time to time. When we feel like we have punished our inner child too harshly, we let loose and allow it to indulge in leisure activities. Then, when we realize that the inner child is having too much fun, our inner parent steps in to enforce some limits.

In this chapter, you will learn how to protect your

inner child in a healthy, balanced manner. But first, let's redefine protection.

Redefine Protection

To "protect" means to shield from harm and injury. But not all harm and injury is detrimental. Not all moments are make-or-break moments. Sometimes, suffering and taking risks are necessary for us to grow and learn. Without failures and mistakes, we don't get to learn from our mistakes and equip ourselves with new skills to deal with challenges in the future. When our inner parent controls the inner child too much by telling it what to do and what not to do, the child's growth and freedom are limited.

Overprotection includes protecting things that do not need to be protected; for example: emotions. Negative emotions such as sorrow and anger might feel unpleasant and overwhelming but they will not destroy us. Overprotecting yourself from emotions makes the nurturing job of your inner parent much harder. The nurturing role is all about validating the feelings of your inner child. If you block your emotions completely, how can the inner child express them?

**The key to protecting your inner child is
to protect without attachment.**

When you are detached, you push your inner child away and avoid taking responsibility for its feelings and behaviors. When you are attached to your inner child, you cling to it and you suffer, too. It's as though you are also a victim. But when you are not attached, you are just there with your inner child. You know how the inner child feels, but you don't lose yourself. You are on standby mode, staying mindful and watching how the whole situation plays out and how your inner child reacts to the situation. Then you respond accordingly.

The main difference between Adam's parents and Betty's parents is that Adam's parents protect him out of fear, and Betty's parents protect her out of love. Adam's parents project a lot of negative energy such as anger and anxiety onto their child, but Betty's parents emanate positive energy such as compassion and kindness. Adam's parents have attached their identities to their son and they can't separate the two. Protecting Adam is more about themselves and their non-acceptance of the situation than it is about their son's well-being. If a car knocks down their son, it's about their loss and the grief they have to go through. If their son doesn't do well in life, it's about their self-image as parents and the shame they might experience. Protecting Adam is partly a means for them to prevent their own negative emotions from getting triggered.

Reflect on this: When your inner child proposes an idea about taking a specific action or expresses its feelings, do you quickly turn it down or ignore it? Ask yourself:

- Is your inner parent projecting its fears and beliefs onto the inner child?
- Is your inner parent afraid that it can't handle the emotions the inner child is bringing forward?
- Is your inner parent protecting its own self-image, or genuinely keeping the inner child away from harm?

Kim Eng, a spiritual teacher, once said in a live seminar that we are so used to hiding ourselves and protecting ourselves that this has become our habit. What we are actually protecting is our ego identity. You might think that you have good intentions because you are protecting your inner child from feeling hurt. But it might just be a case of your inner parent finding it difficult to handle your inner child's pain. You don't know what to do when your inner child makes you aware of its emotional pain, so you would rather not trigger the child. In reality, the inner parent is not protecting the inner child. It's protecting itself.

So does it mean that we just flat out let our inner child get hurt and not protect it at all? Of course, we don't. Non-attachment is not the same as detachment. It doesn't mean you don't care. Of course, you respond when your inner child needs help. We don't expose our inner child's emotional pain and hope that it can handle the pain on its own. Lack of protection is not love, either. The inner child is sensitive and irrational because the overwhelming feelings that are brought forth are based on past events and viewed from the perspective of the child. The inner parent needs to be there to provide guidance and support from an adult perspective. The inner parent needs to say no when appropriate, but also encourage the inner child to try things it is afraid of. This has to be done in a mindful manner so we don't get attached to the inner child's suffering.

To protect our inner child we have to find a balance between the inner child and inner parent. When too much power and control is given to the inner parent, the inner child will feel suffocated. When there is too little guidance from the inner parent, the inner child will wreck havoc. The inner parent has to learn how to respond and not control;

guide and not demand; and support and yet also be non-attached. As challenging as this sounds, it is absolutely necessary for the growth of your inner child and your inner parent.

How Can Your Inner Parent Protect Your Inner Child?

Protection comes in the form of guidance, structure, and discipline, rather than the avoidance of risks and harmful situations.

With guidance and a consistent structure in place, your inner child can navigate the world safely and confidently. On the contrary, if the inner parent removes all risks and obstacles for the inner child, it will have to do it forever. It's like teaching someone how to ride a bicycle. You want to encourage them and catch them if they fall. But you don't want to hold onto the bicycle too tight while they are riding, because then they will not learn how to ride by themselves. They will always depend on you for help.

Furthermore, no matter how well you protect your inner child, there will always be events that will slip through the cracks and trigger its pain. When this happens, the nurturing function of your inner parent will be called upon to help the inner child deal with its emotions. This is the backup when things don't go according to plan. So there's no need to overprotect the inner child. Constantly trying to keep your inner child away from harm will only create unnecessary stress and anxiety.

Below are things your inner parent can do to protect the inner child:

1. Know your inner child's limits and triggers.

Everyone's limit is different. Some people are comfortable with a more direct and aggressive communication style; others might think that talking in such a manner is rude. One person might think that sarcasm is funny, but another might be offended by it.

Your inner parent's job is to determine if another person or a situation is stepping over your inner child's line and making it feel uncomfortable. I cannot tell you what you need to protect your inner child *from*. You have to observe how you feel when you interact with another person or situation to understand your limits and determine what triggers your inner child. This can be done by listening to your body and sensing its reaction to any given situation. You might also need to compare it to similar situations to accurately determine your inner child's limits.

After understanding your inner child's limits and triggers, the inner parent has a decision to make.

**Your inner parent has the choice
to protect or to encourage the inner child.**

For example, if criticism reminds you of the times when your parents criticized you, the inner parent can help you avoid people and situations that have a high likelihood of causing this pain. Alternatively, the inner parent can encourage you to face this pain upfront and not take it personally. It might intentionally seek similar situations to challenge your inner child's limit. Neither one is better than the other. Some emotional pain is too overwhelming to handle at our level of consciousness and it's better to leave these situations alone and process them gradually. But pushing your inner child's limit and helping it overcome its fears and shame can provide much growth for the child.

In my case, I know my father puts me down whenever I share my successes with him, especially if they are related to my creative endeavors. So I usually downplay my success in front of him and not let him know much about my work. If he assumes that I'm doing average in life, I'll let him assume so because there is no need to pick a fight with him. This is how I manage and reduce criticism from my father. I know what triggers my parents' criticism and I don't activate it and feed them with ammunition.

However, there are times when I sense that my inner child is afraid of being rejected by others. At these times, my inner parent encourages it to take the risk. My inner parent will say things like: *Go ahead; you can do it. You'll be fine. I'll be here for you.* Being rejected might make my inner child feel unpleasant, but I know that overcoming fear is good for growth and relationships. So even though I might be nervous in social settings, sometimes I nudge myself a little to open up.

There is no right or definite way. You have to be mindful of what your inner child can or cannot handle and respond skillfully to each situation.

2. Establish external and internal boundaries.

The inner parent has to draw the line and provide structure because the inner child doesn't know how. It has to consult the child and understand what it wants, but it also cannot follow or give in to everything the inner child demands. The child probably has some bad habits, wrong beliefs, and false perceptions that were developed during childhood.

The inner parent needs to provide wisdom and help curb any bad habits.

If you were abused in the past, your inner child might be drawn to situations that allow it to be abused again. It wants to relive the pain you felt as a child. It also might have the illusion that someday the abuser will change. So the inner child might stay in situations that feel familiar, but they don't necessarily benefit from them. The job of the inner parent is to recognize this unhealthy habit and keep the inner child out of situations that allow it to be abused repeatedly. Your inner parent must create external boundaries and learn to say "no" to others. Letting the other party know how you feel and where you stand is part of your inner parent's responsibility.

Kids don't know how to navigate the world they live in. They don't know about rules and regulations. If parents do not teach their kids the necessary rules — for example, *Watch out for cars on the road* and *Don't touch the boiling kettle* — there could be some serious consequences. The inner parent needs to evaluate the needs of the inner child in relation to external reality and decide if a boundary is necessary. It has to observe the external environment and other people and ask: *Is this really dangerous or am I just being overanxious? Will the inner child's desire harm my mind, body, and soul or other people?* If something is truly dangerous or otherwise undesirable, the inner parent has to step in and stop the inner child.

The inner parent also has to set higher standards for the inner child. It has to ask: *What am I not going to settle for? Am I going to put my inner child in an environment where it gets constantly abused or has to deal with people who treat it unkindly?* With practice, the inner parent will get better at determining what's best for the child.

The inner parent needs to balance the inner child's needs with the adult's needs.

Also, sometimes your inner child might want instant gratification. Not only does it want to indulge in emotional pain and relief from the pain, it also wants fun and joy. The inner parent has a totally different agenda. It wants to work and focus on things that matter to adults. Again, neither is right. Both relaxation and work have their merits, depending on the context.

Self-discipline and creating internal boundaries are important. They can help regulate some of the impulses, thoughts, behaviors, and emotions that your inner child might have. When you are working, you wouldn't want to procrastinate or be distracted by your impulses and emotions. Even though it's important to acknowledge our emotions, this doesn't mean they are always true and we need to spend all our time dwelling on them. There is a time to talk about the inner child's problems and a time not to. The inner parent needs to set aside time for work and play, and both your inner child and inner parent need to agree on the schedule.

3. Communicate boundaries clearly and speak kindly to your inner child.

It is even more important for the inner parent to communicate to the child why a boundary is necessary. Some parents assert their rights over their children but never explain their intentions. They allow their kids to assume meanings on their own, and as a consequence, they misunderstand the intentions of their parents.

Whenever your inner parent wants to establish a boundary, make sure the inner child is in agreement. Your inner parent and inner child need to establish mutual understanding so that inner peace can be achieved. If your inner parent forces your inner child to obey without explanation, and without understanding how the child feels, resistance is bound to happen.

Train the inner parent to use kind language rather than criticism.

When you explain your decision to the inner child, you are making your intentions known to the child and you are also creating an opportunity to clarify any doubts. Unlike criticism, you are not forcing your views on your inner child. You want to have a balance of power between your inner child and your inner parent. But once you use criticism or force, the balance of power will be in favor of the inner parent, as though it is telling the inner child what to do. The inner parent then becomes the inner critic and you don't want that to happen. If there is any resistance from your inner child, you have to reconcile the differences before moving forward.

Sometimes, it's more meaningful to lead by example. The inner child probably did not have a good role model to learn from while growing up. If the inner parent is able to be a good role model for the inner child, the child will naturally trust the inner parent's way of doing things. But again, you have to make your intentions clear and consult the inner child's feelings before you act.

4. Let go of control.

The more you try to control your inner child's impulses, the more resistance you will experience inside of yourself. Sometimes, you just have to let go of control because when your inner parent tries to control your inner child, the child will be controlling it at the same time.

Just like when we grow up and have our own identity, parents who can't accept that their children have changed and have formed their own identity are going to feel miserable. Only when they let go and accept the changes in their children will they find peace and be able to create harmonious relationships.

Letting go doesn't mean you don't care anymore.

To let go means to allow your children to grow and learn on their own. Sometimes, it might be more effective for us to act on our inner child's impulses, make mistakes, and then provide the necessary guidance. In this way, the inner child will learn how impulsive behavior can lead to unfavorable outcomes, and they will try to avoid making the same mistake again. This is better than telling your inner child what to do and what not to do. People usually resist being told what to do.

This also applies to the inner parent. If the parent has a strong desire to do something, it might be better to simply go ahead and see what happens. If it turns out to be a mistake, the inner parent can apologize to the inner child, and we can learn from it, too.

Finally, as mentioned before, whatever the protective function of the inner parent fails to do, the nurturing function will be there to pick up the pieces. So let's understand what the nurturing function of the inner parent entails.

Chapter 6

Nurture the Inner Child

"Whatever happens to you belongs to you. Make it yours. Feed it to yourself even if it feels impossible to swallow. Let it nurture you, because it will."

— CHERYL STRAYED, TINY BEAUTIFUL THINGS

All children need unconditional love from their parents. They need attention, approval, understanding, acceptance, warmth, and affection. In the same way, the inner parent can nurture the inner child. This function complements the protective aspect of the inner parent. When the inner child is experiencing overwhelming emotions, you can help the child feel better by showing it empathy. When the inner child makes mistakes or breaks boundaries, the inner parent is there to forgive the inner child. The parent is not only there to listen to the child's problems, it also has to create an environment that is safe enough for the child to open up and talk about its feelings. The nurturing function is about creating trust with the inner child. But can a parent be over-nurturing?

Over-nurturance is usually tied with not providing enough structure and consistency. I've seen parents give in to their children's demands too easily. When their children ask for something, they simply provide it, even though they know it won't be good for the children in the long run. Sometimes, they try to impose limits on their children, but often they are not firm and consistent with these limits. After some pleading and guilt-tripping, the parents usually give in to the demands of their children.

Nurture without ego.
Give up your image of being a good parent.

Both overprotecting and over-nurturing are not acts of love. Often times, the parents just want to protect their image of being good parents. It's more about feeding their ego and identity than doing what's best for their children. I used to have a young student who whenever I asked her to solve mathematical questions would say something negative about me: *You are a bad teacher; you are mean;* or *you are boring.* It was very tempting to give in to her requests to play instead of study because my ego wanted to maintain a good image. But I realized that she was trying to make me feel guilty so she would have fewer math problems to solve. So I said, "Even if I'm a bad teacher, we still have to do the questions." She became frustrated because she couldn't control me, and eventually I had to let her go. But at least I kept to my limits and was true to my responsibilities. I wasn't hired to play with her. I was supposed to help her with her studies.

When parents nurture their children too much, the children feel entitled. It's as though the whole world revolves around them. When our inner parent nurtures the inner child too much, we might end up being overly self-absorbed. Yes, when your inner child has problems or requests, your inner parent has to be there to listen and give it attention. But if your whole consciousness revolves around the inner child, you will be so bogged down by the child's emotional needs — or the fun the child wants to have —that you can't do anything else, and your adult life will suffer as a result.

On the contrary, if your inner parent does not give your inner child enough attention, love, and empathy, it will seek love and approval elsewhere from some external person or thing. Then, you will always have to depend on others to satisfy your needs.

The Importance of Self-Approval

Do you find yourself looking for approval all the time? I used to look to my parents for approval. But when I stopped seeking their approval, I realized I subconsciously started looking for approval elsewhere. For example, when I asked my mentor a question, I wasn't really interested in his answers to my questions. I was seeking his affirmations and permission to do the things I wanted to do.

Seeking approval from others means you are asking them for their opinions and permission to do something. It means you want to be accepted by them. But when you ask others for permission, there's a risk that you will be rejected and criticized. If your parents are constantly criticizing you, ask yourself: *Do I constantly seek approval from my parents, giving them an opportunity to criticize and reject me?*

What child doesn't want their parents to approve of them and accept them? But, unfortunately, not all parents support the choices their kids make. As adults, we are responsible for our own choices, regardless of whether or not our parents approve of them. When we were children, our survival depended on our parents. If we didn't get their approval, we risked not being loved and taken care of. But this is not the case now that we are grown up.

> **Self-approval is more important than the approval of someone else, including your parents.**

Even if your parents disagree with our adult choices, what's stopping us from moving ahead? The reason their disapproval has so much emotional charge for us is we believe they are still in control of us. But no, they do not control their adult children. If you don't care whether your parents disapprove of you or your choices, then don't ask for their opinions, especially if you have controlling parents. This just gives them more opportunities to criticize you.

Don't expect your parents to give you the approval and recognition you want so badly. This might sound a bit disheartening, but having an expectation like this is going be disappointing. Instead, always give yourself the approval first. Let your parents' approval be a bonus, not something you seek.

Whenever I catch myself wanting to tell my parents

how well or bad my choices turned out, I know that my inner child needs some form of approval and love. Instead of depending on my actual parents, it's my inner parent's duty to direct empathy inward and give my inner child some attention.

Often times, we seek love outside of ourselves, hoping that other people will give us the love we want. But other people might not be in touch with their own loving presence and so they are unable to provide us with the love we need. We must go deeper and connect with our loving presence within. In this way, we can provide ourselves with the love we need. As mentioned in my book, *Empty Your Cup*, not only do we have an abundance of love within, we are the source of love. As long as we are connected to our spiritual self, we will be able to feel the unwavering love that is always within us. The inner parent needs to know how to tap into this source of love, instead of seeking external validation to satisfy the inner child.

How to Develop the Trust of Your Inner Child Through Listening

Trust is important. Without it, you don't know how you authentically feel about anything, including other people.

But it's not easy to get your inner child to show its true colors, especially if your inner parent has done something to hurt the child in the past. For example, your inner parent might have been too critical of your inner child or performed self-harming activities such as drinking too much alcohol or over-working in order to stop your inner child from showing its emotions.

Here are some suggestions you can follow to encourage your inner child to trust your inner parent again and express its needs more freely:

1. Let go of your parental pride.

As a tutor, I have to be careful not to let my pride or ego get in the way of listening to my students. I don't always know more than my students. The students might have learned easier methods from their schoolteacher or there might be a syllabus change that I'm not aware of. Plus, sometimes I make mistakes, too. So I have to learn as much as I teach.

We can never know more than the other person.

If I get too carried away with my pride as a teacher and think that I know more than my students, then I will not be fully there to listen to what they have to say. Most parents decide what's best for their children, instead of consulting the children and asking them what they want. Like in my case, my dad believes that putting us down will make us more grounded and less conceited. He thinks it's good for us. But that's not what I needed as a child. I don't need to be praised every day. However, I do need some affirmation to tell me that I'm doing well and some acknowledgment for my effort.

Your knowledge and belief of what is good for your inner child keeps you from learning and understanding the child. If you really want to find out the needs of your inner child, you have to ask your inner parent to step back a little so the child has a chance to talk.

The best place to start is to tell the inner child: *I don't know; please tell me more.*

2. Listen with an open mind.

Some children behave very differently in front of their parents and other people. They adopt a fake persona in front of their parents for the sake of survival. It's a pity that parents don't ever get to see how their kids truly feel.

I used to teach young children. They always appeared to be obedient and subservient in front of their parents. However, some of them behaved totally different when their parents weren't around. One time, I had a student who said: "I hate my mom! She must be inside the room playing on her iPad. Yet, she doesn't let me play."

On the surface, children might obey their parents. But it doesn't change the fact that they are resentful inside. Do you really want fake obedience? Do you want your inner child to obey the rules you have set for it, but secretly do things that sabotage your effort?

Let go of judgment
so your inner child can be honest with you.

To approach your inner child, you must come with an open mind, even if the child tells you something that sounds ridiculous. Let go of your judgment. Don't say things like, *Get over it. It will never work. It doesn't matter.* Don't judge your inner child when it brings you back to the past. Just ask the child what it needs and what is it feeling in the present. Ask questions instead of making statements. As irrational as the feelings might be, your inner child can provide valuable information about your habitual actions and behaviors. So don't dismiss what they have to say.

The reason why children stop talking to their parents is that the parents don't value their opinions. Your inner child wants to feel accepted by your inner parent. If you want your inner child to be open with you, you must encourage the child to express his or her feelings and respect those feelings. Be open to listening and accepting whatever is communicated. Develop a good relationship with your inner child, and it will share everything with you. Brush it aside, and you will never be able to find out how the child truly feels.

3. Admit your mistakes and apologize.

The inner child holds a lot of pain, not just from your birth parents but also from your inner parent. If you have done anything to hurt yourself previously, apologize to your inner child. Even if it's something your birth parents did and it's not your fault, apologize for not being there or being strong enough to protect your inner child. You can also apologize for taking so long to recognize and understand your inner child's pain.

**Your inner child is waiting
for a genuine, heartfelt apology.**

Your parents might never tell you they are sorry, and your inner child might never get the apology it yearns for.

So why not take the initiative and say *I'm sorry* to the child? Regardless of where the apology comes from, as long as it's genuine your inner child will feel a sense of relief. Your inner child wants the hardship and pain it endures to be recognized. An apology will soften the feeling of indignation the child has been holding on to for so long and allow the child to be more genuine.

Also, don't cover up for your inner parent when it makes a mistake. Own up, take responsibility, and apologize. Your inner parent is not always right or more valuable than your inner child. They each have their own purpose. Treat all subpersonalities the same and your inner child will naturally trust you more.

4. Be present with your inner child.

Being there for your inner child shows that you love the child. The inner child needs your time and attention. When the child is being reminded of something from the past and has difficulty dealing with certain emotions, your inner parent needs to comfort and calm it down. If you do this often enough, not only will your inner child feel safe to communicate with you, it will also feel loved and understood.

**When your baby is crying, don't leave it alone.
Pick it up and show that you care.**

On the contrary, if your inner parent is always too busy and ignores your inner child when it calls for help, eventually the child will stop asking for help and you will never find out what your inner child truly needs. When the child stops crying, you might think that it's great, because you can finally concentrate on your work. What you don't realize is that your inner child has numbed itself so much that it feels helpless to even cry for help. *What's the use of crying for help when you know that no one will be there to help you?* Once you have reached this stage, it becomes very difficult to get in touch with your emotions again. You lose a lot of valuable information about your habitual actions and behaviors when you disconnect from your inner child.

I get it. When you are working, you don't want your emotions to get in the way. But it doesn't take a lot of time to soothe your inner child and show that you care. Especially when you are mindful, your inner child will naturally be affected by your peaceful presence. Simply pause and listen. You can also ask questions using a gentle tone, if necessary, such as: *Why do you feel this way?* Or acknowledge your inner child by saying things such as *I hear you* and *I love you.*

During my episode of depression, I noticed that the left side of my arm often felt a cold pang. Now that my depression is gone, whenever I feel fear or sorrow, my left hand, especially my left thumb, feels cold. Intuitively, I soothe this part of my body by holding my left thumb with my right hand. As a result, I feel much better, more comfortable, and calmer. I'm not sure if there is a name for this technique, but you are welcome to try my method.

Pain is experienced in the body. We might not remember our childhood trauma, but the body remembers the pain and the events that caused it. *The Body Keeps the Score: Brain, Mind, and Body in the Healing of Trauma* by Bessel van der Kolk and *Waking the Tiger: Healing Trauma* by Peter A. Levine and Ann Frederick discuss this topic in detail.

You don't have to get lost in your inner child's emotions or do anything tangible to solve the problem. Just be there when the child needs a pillar to lean on. This already means a lot to the child.

Balancing the Protective and Nurturing Functions

Finding the balance between the protective and nurturing

functions is not easy. If you set too strict a limit without showing love for your inner child, the child will not trust you enough to share its emotional pain with you. It might sabotage your efforts subconsciously and be unwilling to cooperate or follow the rules that your inner parent has set. When your rules are met with resistance, you might find that it's even worse than having no rules at all.

However, if you nurture your inner child excessively without having any boundaries, you can get sucked into the inner child's stories. You might end up spending days reliving past memories and emotions and lose touch with the present moment. You might also be led down a path by your inner child that you will regret later.

Mindfulness helps bring
the two elements together.

To create a balance between the protective and nurturing functions, you need to have a certain level of awareness and mindfulness. Bringing in the spiritual self (the observer) will help you become aware of the imbalance between the two functions. When you realize that your rules and limits are being met with resistance, it's time for the inner parent to lower its focus on the ego and spend some time understanding why the inner child is resisting so much. If you realize that the emotions and old pains the child is bringing to your awareness are too much for you to handle, you will need to be present and take a step back from the stories. In essence, your spiritual self is the inner guidance and love that your inner parent can rely on to protect and nurture the inner child.

Now that we have equipped our inner parent with the skills to love and care for our inner child, it's time to delve a little deeper and help the child heals its childhood pains.

PART 3

Healing the Inner Child

Chapter 7

Uncover Your Childhood Pain

*"We cultivate love when we allow our most vulnerable
and powerful selves to be deeply seen and known."*

— BRENÉ BROWN, THE GIFTS OF IMPERFECTION

*This is probably the fifteenth time I have rehearsed for the video
presentation, so why am I still feeling emotional and getting
teary?* I thought to myself.

In September 2015, at the same entrepreneur program
as mentioned in Chapter 4, we were given the assignment
to shoot two videos about our business. Since I didn't have
a business and I wasn't clear about the type of business I
was going to manifest, I decided to shoot two videos for my
book, *Fearless Passion*. One of the videos would be a book
trailer and the other would be a short parable about the
moon that was included in the book. I didn't have any

problem with the first video. I was able to come up quickly with the script, the storyboard, and the shots needed for the trailer. However, when it came to the second video, I kept getting stuck.

The moon parable was written about a decade ago when I felt melancholy and lonely one night while looking at the moon. In the video, I wanted to share how I came to write the story and my experiences of having low self-esteem in secondary school. But whenever I talked about how I felt neglected by my peers in school, and how I assured my mom that everything was fine even though it was not, I choked up and couldn't continue.

It didn't make any sense. These incidents were already in the past. *It all happened almost two decades ago, so why am I still affected? Didn't I let go of these incidents? Should I do this video or not?* I was worried, but still thinking that I could overcome my emotions eventually, I continued with the rehearsals.

The day came when we were supposed to record our videos. It was nerve-wracking because I didn't realize that there would be so many people watching me shoot the video. The first video went smoothly, as expected. I just needed to read off a script that I had prepared previously. But the audience stayed on to watch the second video.

What am I going to do?

Taking a deep breath, I began to regurgitate what I remembered. But halfway through the video, I started sobbing uncontrollably *again*. I felt more emotional than during my rehearsals. I hadn't cried like this in front of so many people since I was a primary school kid. *What is wrong with me? Why can't I stop my tears? Haven't I cried enough already?* The more I resisted crying, the more I sobbed. The audience was stunned by my display of emotion and didn't know how to react. But the cameraman, who was my friend, showed no signs of stopping and neither did my tears. So I continued and completed the video, half-sobbing, and half-talking.

At the end of the video, I felt embarrassed yet relieved. It was supposed to be a business video, but it ended up becoming a public therapy session for me. As a result, I received pure love, support, and empathy from my friends. They thought I was courageous and authentic to share my story and vulnerability. Some of them could relate to what I shared, and they told me they had similar feelings about themselves in the past.

Looking back now, I don't know why I did that video. There were so many other topics I could have chosen. But I guess it was probably time for me to uncover some of the pain I had been avoiding for so long.

The Well-Protected Wound

Can you recall most of the things in your childhood? Are there blank spaces in your memory or experiences you don't want to remember or talk about?

When people are asked about their childhood, some either don't remember much or they can only remember the positive and happy memories. Yes, our inner child has a side that is happy, fun, and playful. But more often than not, it also holds on to a lot of hurt feelings and suffering from the past. It's just that we might have forgotten about them or unconsciously blocked them out. People who have suffered from traumatic events and abuse in childhood might not remember exactly what happened to them. Their brains have repressed these painful memories for protection and to help them cope with life. They believe that if they allow these disturbing images or emotions to surface, they won't be able to deal with them.

Our inner parent has instructed our inner child not to express its pain.

Our inner parent doesn't want us to get hurt.

Unfortunately, denying and suppressing our emotional pain is not a good way to resolve it. In the midst of protection, it also ignores the needs of the inner child. This leaves the child with no choice but to express its pain through subtle, sabotaging means, such as those mentioned in Chapter 2, or through an emotional outburst like what happened during my video recording.

In my case, even though I could clearly remember the past events in school, I hadn't allowed myself to process my emotions properly. It was more like: *Okay, those things were in the past. They are over. I can see why I felt left out in school and why young children behave in such a manner. But now that I'm an adult, I'm fine.* There hasn't been any acknowledgment of the emotions and hardship I went through as a teen. In other words, I have not allowed myself to completely feel the feelings that have always been there, stored by my inner child.

When we were young, we didn't know how to handle our emotional wounds. Instead of treating them immediately, we covered them up. Kids cover their eyes when they see something frightening. Out of sight, out of mind, right? As we grow up, our inner parent adds more and more layers of protection until the pain is nowhere to be found.

Our inner child has suffered a lot, but we can't recognize its pain. The pain is buried deep down inside our subconscious, where is it well-protected by the inner parent. It's like putting a bandage on an untreated wound. I've been removing layers and layers of protection without realizing that the wound is still unhealed under the bandage. When I'm close to removing the last layer of the bandage, I can see the pain that I have been ignoring for so long and I am scared of my rising, intense emotions.

We can choose to ignore our inner child and its pain, but that doesn't mean the wound is not there or that it is fully healed. The wounds still exist and the inner child is still waiting for us to remove the defenses and heal its wounds.

Removing the Bandages Layer by Layer

Once my writer friend wasn't sure if she was emotionally ready to write her memoir because she is still feeling the pain and shedding tears over it. My reply to her was, "You can never be emotionally ready for pain. Otherwise, it wouldn't be called *pain.*"

It takes courage to face your pain, and I understand it's not easy. Our mind makes us think that we are not strong enough to handle the pain. But if you are not in touch with the pain, or you do not cry the tears that you are supposed to have cried when you were a child, the emotions will always be trapped in your body and they will dictate your actions and behaviors. Furthermore, we are not meant to keep our emotions inside. It can lead to mental or other chronic, physical illnesses. Don't underestimate the impact that suppressed emotions can cause.

Your pain needs to be recognized and acknowledged.

It needs to be acknowledged and then released. Avoiding pain is the same as denying it. You don't have to share your past with other people if you are afraid of being judged or if it makes you feel uncomfortable. You also don't have to face your pain all at once. When injured people remove their bandages, they do it slowly and gingerly, layer by layer. They don't rip off their bandages all at once. Sometimes, they also need help from doctors and nurses.

If you are revisiting your childhood wounds for the first time after a long time, or you had an especially traumatic childhood, it might not be wise to crack open all your defenses at once by yourself. Some of us might not be able to handle the intense emotions that have been hiding below the surface and that could be potentially dangerous, especially those of us who haven't been practicing mindfulness. We might need someone who is mindful and compassionate, such as a spiritual teacher or a therapist to help and guide us.

Healing our childhood pain takes time and multiple sessions of letting go. We are so good at protecting our emotional pain that we don't realize it has become significant. Understanding the different protective mechanisms your inner parent has put in place will help you remove the defenses one by one, layer by layer, so you can reach the depth of your emotional pain and release it.

Here are four protective layers that your inner parent might have adopted to mask your hurt feelings.

Layer 1: Denial

What pain? There's no pain at all. I had a happy childhood. Denial is a layer of defense that is the toughest to crack open. If a person doesn't recognize that they are still holding on to pain, how does he or she release it?

Denial comes in many forms. As mentioned previously, some of us have repressed memories. We don't remember our childhood experiences and the suffering we have been through. Others might remember their unhappy experiences but choose to ignore them. For the rest of us, denial might come in the form of devaluing the importance of our pain and numbing the intensity of the pain. Deep down inside, we know the pain is there but we brush it aside and pretend it doesn't exist or it's insignificant.

Whether we do it intentionally or unconsciously, denying our childhood pain helps us avoid our past and not feel our uncomfortable emotions again. But not being aware of your emotional wounds doesn't mean they are not there. By denying our pain, we can end up getting stuck at this stage for a very long time.

Remedy denial with authenticity.

Have you come across people who said they are not angry or upset with you even though they sounded angry and upset when they talked to you? Many of us are brought up to believe that it's not good to express or have feelings. When children cry, what do most parents do? They ask their children to stop crying. Seldom, you will see a parent acknowledging the children's emotions. Most of us are taught to deny our emotions growing up, making it easy to lose touch with them.

To remove this protective layer, you have to be authentic with all your feelings. If you feel angry about something, you have to acknowledge the existence of the anger. This doesn't mean you have to act on your feelings, but it's important to admit to yourself that you have such feelings.

One good thing that came out of my experience of returning to my previous company is that I have become more aware and accepting of my feelings. In the past, I would continue with my job and try to cope with the nagging, unhappy voice in my head. This time around, I was able to be more open with how I felt and I told everyone how stressed I was at my job. Instead of pretending that I'm fine and upholding the image that I can do anything, I felt a sense of relief at being honest with my emotions, not just in front of others but more importantly in front of myself.

Layer 2: Anger

When we recognize that our childhood was not as pleasant as we thought it was, most of us feel some level of anger and resentment about the situation or our parents. Similar to denial, these emotions protect us from feeling hurt.

When we blame someone else for our experiences, we are focusing on the other person, not on ourselves. We divert our attention away from our emotional wounds.

Let's look at anger first. Anger carries so much energy with it. It's hard to ignore unless you are someone like me who has been used to numbing their anger since they were young. For most, it is easier to manage anger and rage than painful emotions such as shame and fear. It's easier to be mad at another person than to be mad at ourselves. Some of us would rather have an estranged relationship with our parents than feel unworthy and powerless in their presence. But anger is just a cover-up for other emotions.

Beneath anger, there are hurt feelings.

We can leave our parents and hate them for making our childhood miserable, but it won't make us feel better. Even though our anger might have subsided when our parents are not around, it can still be easily triggered by other situations that resemble our childhood experiences. If you felt neglected as a child or were heavily criticized by your parents, you will feel the same when others ignore or criticize you. It doesn't matter if your parents are still here or not. Someone else can make you feel the same way when they trigger the pain your inner child carries.

Under every feeling of anger, there are feelings of neglect, shame, being unloved, misunderstood, and fear. I realized the anger that I had for my job was just my inner child's way of expressing his constant fear of not being good enough. He believed that he couldn't meet the deadlines and do the work on time. Not only was he afraid of disappointing others, he didn't want to risk failing and feeling flawed in front of them. Once I was able to delve deeper, understand how my inner child feels, and show him compassion, the anger I was feeling dissolved into anxiety (which is really what's hiding behind the anger). I was then able to deal with my fear accordingly and concentrate on my work.

Layer 3: Resentment

For those of us who are not in touch with our anger, we mostly end up feeling resentful. Resentment is a distant relative of anger. They are similar, except that resentment is more persistent and carries less energy than anger. We will resent our parents if we feel they treated us unfairly and that we deserved better. However, instead of communicating our feelings directly, we let our indignation fester under the surface and we become passive-aggressive.

Even though we might love our parents, we also blame them for not giving us the love we yearned for as children, and also now that we are adults.

This resentment toward our parents has a long history. As a child, some of us might have tried to change ourselves to please them. Our parents are the closest relations we have in this world, and we want to have a good relationship with them. We try to fulfill their expectations, based on our interpretation of what we believe will make them love us. If we believe that our parents like us to be quiet, we will do our best to stay quiet. If we believe our parents will praise us when we get good grades, we study hard to attain the praise. Deep down inside, we want our parents to be proud of us and love us unconditionally.

However, some of us realized that our parents couldn't be pleased. Either they had too high an expectation of us, or they expected us to do something that we were not capable of doing. For example, if you have ADHD and were not diagnosed early, you probably went through a period of time when your parents sat you down and expected you to do your homework quietly, but you were restless and could not sit still. This likely created a lot of misunderstanding between you and your parents. This is also true when you have different personality traits than your parents. Perhaps you are an introvert and love to stay at home, but they want you to be more outgoing and interact with the other kids. Maybe you are empathetic and sensitive, but your parents detest the expression of emotions and want you to be tough. They might want you to be something that isn't natural to you.

Resentment helps mask our feeling that we are not accepted by our parents.

Most of us don't want to resent our parents. But our resentment starts to grow when they constantly invalidate our sense of self. We can't help but complain or blame them for being overly critical, narcissistic, and controlling. Some of us might also believe that our parents treat our siblings, their work, or themselves better than they treat us.

On the surface, we appear to feel disappointed and bitter. We tried so hard to please them and change their opinions of us, but nothing seemed to work. At the core of us, there is a deep pain because our parents never accepted us, even though we have looked to them for love and approval since we were quite young.

Layer 4: Self-Blame

Some people use anger to avoid feeling bad about themselves, while the rest of us use self-blame to numb our anger toward our parents. Instead of directing our anger externally toward our parents, we direct the anger internally toward ourselves.

Growing up, we thought we were the cause of our parents' actions or we deserved to be treated unkindly by them. For example, our justification might be that they criticized or punished us for our own good. We believed that we weren't good enough, so we needed to be disciplined harshly by them. Perhaps when our enabler parent did nothing to save us from the abuse and trauma caused by the abusive parent, we thought we were not lovable or important enough for the enabler parent to do anything about it. We might even blame ourselves for not protecting ourselves, escaping, or doing something about our traumatic experiences, even though we were only children and had no ability to protect ourselves or get away.

Some of us were also raised to believe that it's inappropriate to be angry with others, especially our parents. We feel guilty for being angry with them. So we defend their behaviors with reasons and rationalization, and blame ourselves instead.

Self-blame is where many of our hurt feelings reside, but there is something more.

Even deeper than the shame we feel about ourselves, are the feelings of fear and grief. As children, we were afraid that if we were not good enough our parents would not love us anymore and they would leave us. Probably more hurtful was the thought that they never loved us in the first place and never will. Our parents are supposed to love us, but often they hurt us, whether intentionally or unintentionally. This realization of our loss of parental love is so devastating that we would rather blame ourselves for their inability to love us.

Self-blame is a very convenient way to explain our parents' actions and misdirect our fear and grief. As long as we know the reason why they behave the way they do, we will have something to work on and please them. If you think you are unlovable or unimportant, you will assume you need to do the things you believe will make your parents love or notice you. There is a path to getting your needs met.

On the flip side, if you have no idea why your parents treat you the way they do, you will be constantly living in fear and depression. There is nothing you can do to get love from your parents. If your dreams of being loved are dashed and there is no clear path to getting your needs met, you are likely to feel hopeless and powerless. This is why our minds find us something to work on. Whether it's the right or wrong perception is beside the point.

Essentially, we are using blame to protect ourselves from feeling our innate fear and grief as children. It's still a protective layer and we don't stop here.

As the Pain Is Being Exposed

As you uncover your childhood pain, you might find it challenging to remove your protective mechanisms. Most people are not willing to go to the fourth layer because it can be the most painful. If you are not mindful and careful, you can easily get sucked into your past and end up dwelling and indulging in it — and losing yourself in self-blame and victimhood. Perhaps, like what happened to me, you could lose control over your emotions and have a breakdown. This is why most people avoid the fourth layer. They would rather stay at the layer of denial, anger, and resentment because it feels more comfortable and safe.

However, if you are able to go deeper into your feelings, you will find that the pain isn't as horrible as you imagined it to be. When you have been walking through a dark tunnel for a long time, the first ray of sunlight is going to hurt your eyes. But if you continue on the path despite your initial discomfort, you will soon find the exit.

Emotions are energy. When you are working through your pain, you might find that your emotions can be felt intensively in some parts of your body. For example, when I was in fear, I discovered that my left hand trembled, and when I was feeling angry, my chest would tighten. Being aware of these inner bodily sensations and tensions can help you lessen the intensity of the pain. It also tells you exactly where in your body self-soothing is needed so that you can calm these parts down accordingly. There are several self-soothing methods you can adopt such as tapping, stroking, and holding the bodily parts where the emotions feel the strongest. Just imagine how you would calm down a crying baby and do the same for yourself. Once these emotions are processed, you will feel much better.

Self-compassion arises naturally after you remove the layer of self-blame and negative perceptions of yourself.

When you are blaming yourself, it's hard to find any compassion for yourself. But when you recognize that your negative perception of yourself is just a protective layer and your self-judgment is false, it's much easier to develop compassion for yourself. Instead of thinking that you are worthless, you will realize that you are *afraid* of being perceived as worthless in front of your parents. Like all children, you are scared of losing your parents' love and being disconnected from them. Once you know that all of us experienced some sort of fear and powerlessness as a child, and it's not your fault, you will have more compassion toward yourself.

Mindfulness helps you create a space between you and your inner child.

Mindfulness is key in avoiding getting dragged into a downward spiral and becoming lost in drama from the past. You need to be fully aware that the emotions, tears, and suffering you are experiencing in the present are a product of your past memories. It's not who you are right now. You are not your inner child anymore. You are just allowing it to express and process its long forgotten and neglected feelings.

When you are mindful, the tears you cry will be tears of compassion and empathy for your inner child. They are not tears of victimhood and despair. There is a space between you and the child. You might feel sad that you had to go through so many negative experiences when you were young, but you will realize you are not that past self any longer.

It's all about being open and curious. When you revisit your childhood experiences, examine them with curiosity instead of resistance. Allow all the emotions you have been holding back for so long to surface and observe them. If you haven't been feeling the pain for all these years, it's understandable that you might need to spend some time there and process the emotion several times. When you perceive something that appears to be inaccurate or dubious, it's a good opportunity to clarify it with your parents or siblings, too.

Chapter 8

End the Blame Game

"There is an expiry date on blaming your parents for steering you in the wrong direction; the moment you are old enough to take the wheel, responsibility lies with you."

— J.K. ROWLING

What do the three layers of protection: anger, resentment, and self-blame have in common? Blame. We hold someone else, or ourselves, responsible for some difficulty or fault in order to avoid feeling the inner child's pain.

Our mind is quick to find someone to blame. It assigns a reason for everything that happens, and it needs to find the cause of our problems so we can take action. Once a troublemaker has been assigned, we can then decide how to avoid, solve, or eliminate the problem. This is our basic survival instinct. Human beings are constantly attuned to threats and dangers, and we might blame others more often than we realize. For example, when we try to change our parents, give them the cold shoulder, or cut off contact with them, we give out the energy that they are at fault and they need to do something about it. Even though we might not have verbally blamed them, we indirectly do so with our actions and behaviors.

Blaming doesn't take away the pain.
It keeps the pain intact.

Blames imply directs our attention away from our pain and on to another person. It might seem as though we feel better when we blame someone else. But the truth is the hurt feelings still linger. They are just hidden out of sight and avoided.

Blame gives out an aggressive, demanding energy. When you blame someone, it's as good as saying: *You cause me to suffer. It's your fault. I'm right. You're wrong. Apologize now.* Once a person blames another, he or she has started the blaming game. Someone will have to accept the blame for the game to stop. To do this, the person's ego will have to shrink a little, and whose ego would want to do that?

The blaming game is endless. Pride keeps us from

accepting blame and apologizing to others. When you blame another person, what usually happens is it automatically triggers the other person's ego to defend against your accusation to protect its positive identity. If you attack a positive trait that the other person holds dear, it will be seen as an immediate threat to their self-image. They are naturally going to deflect the blame back to you or attribute it to someone or something else.

The Endless Blaming Game

When You Blame Your Parents

In general, it's hard for any parent to accept blame from their children. After all, they spent so many years and so much money raising you. Your accusations will cause them to feel betrayed. They probably see themselves as good parents, or at least decent ones. Their egos will not let them believe they are capable of doing something that hurts their child. To accept the blame is as good as killing the good parental image they have of themselves. Your parents might not want to talk about how they have hurt you, or they might pretend that some destructive incident never happened because of the negative emotions they will experience might be too unbearable.

Furthermore, parents might find it difficult to understand and accept that they are at fault. If you have strict parents, they might not even perceive their criticism or punishment as something wrong or hurtful. If they did, they would have stopped. Most of them think they are doing you a favor by pointing out your mistakes and disciplining you. Some parents might not even remember what they did, because (unlike you) the event didn't leave a deep impression on them.

Once you blame someone for something, only you or the other party can resolve the blame.

When you blame your parents, you are actually giving your power away. You are letting them decide if they want to accept responsibility, or not. If they are not reflective, you will end up chasing an apology that you are never going to get. To resolve your pain, most likely you will be required to end the blame game. You have to be in touch with your own anger and hurt feelings, and then let them go. If this is not possible, you will have to be the one to let go of your pride and ask for help... from your parents.

In the book, *The Art of Communicating*, the Buddhist monk, Thich Nhat Hanh, mentions the fourth mantra of loving speech: "I suffer, please help." This is such a simple mantra, but yet it's so difficult to execute because of our pride. He goes on to explain: "We want to show the other person that without him or her we can survive very well. This is an indirect way of saying, "I don't need you." But that's not true. In fact, when we suffer, we need others, but we usually do the opposite."

When your parents hurt you, instead of suffering alone or blaming them you can be gentler with your approach. You can say something like this: "I cherish our relationship, but I felt hurt by your actions. I can't let it go and I need your help to heal my pain. I don't understand why you did or said what you did. Please explain and help me understand." This gives out a much different vibe than blaming the other person. Your parents are more likely to respond in a kindly manner and clear up any misunderstanding.

When Your Parents Blame You

Sometimes, one or both of your parents start the blame game and you unwittingly participate in it. For example, your parents might blame you for making them unhappy because you don't do what they told you to do. To prevent our ego from hurting, most of us will deflect the blame by accusing our parents of being too controlling, not understanding, etc.

Ideally, the best person to end the blame game is the person who started it. But what if your parents are not conscious enough to do this. What can you do?

The first step is to let go of any judgment you might have about your parents and not get involved in the blame game. Your parents' accusations might irritate or annoy you, but they are neither good nor bad people. Their views are neither right nor wrong.

There is no right or wrong in a relationship, just different perspectives, beliefs, and worldviews.

Everyone's perception is different. We are all "right" based on our own reality and perception. Take a singing competition, for example. Two judges can watch the same performance and yet have very different opinions. One might like it, and the other might not. Both are right, based on their own preferences and their knowledge of what a good song is, but neither of their judgments is the absolute truth. The performance is neither good nor bad; it can only be good or bad from the judge's point of view. If someone wins the competition, it just means the judges, as a collective whole, favor this performance more than the others. It doesn't mean that everyone enjoyed the performance.

In most cases, it's difficult to judge who is right or wrong. When your parents scold or hit you with good intentions, are they right or wrong? When your parents felt hurt by your actions or inaction, even if you never intended to hurt them, the truth is they are suffering. So are they right to blame you for their suffering?

The second step is to not accept blame from your parents. In other words, don't blame yourself for making your parents unhappy and feel guilty and ashamed about it. It doesn't mean that you don't need to reflect on your actions, try to understand their point of view, or do something to ease the situation. But know you did the best you could with the awareness you had at the time and you are not responsible for your parents' happiness, they are.

Take my parents, for example. They believe that having a stable job will make me happy. But from my perspective, this is not what I want in life. Even though their intention is good, it makes me unhappy to follow their suggestions. I can share my perspectives with them all day long, but I can't help them deal with their emotions, manage their expectations of me, and accept the situation.

As much as it pains me to see them suffer, ultimately, *only* they can relieve themselves from their suffering.

The ego needs to determine who is right and who is wrong, but our true self doesn't.

Wanting to be right will not provide you with resolution. When someone blames you, refuse to accept the aggressive *energy* that blaming brings and avoid the urge to find someone else to blame. If you accept the energy and feel wronged by your parents, you are letting the aggressive energy spread in your body. The anger in you will most likely rise up to deflect the blame back to your parents and the blaming game will continue. But if you don't accept the blame, the aggressive energy will have nothing to feed on and will diffuse on its own.

For example, if your parents blame you for making a mess of the house and you are not the one who did it, you can let them know and still clean the house. You don't have to resent them for having a wrong perception about you. This is what happened to me one day at the restroom. The cleaner accused me of littering. I said it wasn't me. Then I picked up the litter and left the restroom. I could have argued with him, resented him the whole day, and felt indignant about the accusation. But instead, I chose to not accept the accusation and the energy he directed at me. I chose not to let the incident ruin my day.

Why Forgive?

If neither party stops the blaming game, the relationship usually ends up being estranged. Both parties stop talking to each other. On the surface, both parties seem apathetic toward each other, but they are actually still holding onto hurt feelings.

It's not always easy to forgive someone and let go of blame, especially when your parents are not there to explain or apologize for their actions. In that case, how are you going to gain new perspectives and forgive them?

Before we talk about *how* to forgive, it's important to understand *why* forgiveness is essential. Many people have the misconception that when we forgive someone, we are doing it for the other person. We think the other person intends to hurt us, but by letting them off the hook we are supporting their wrong actions and letting them get away with a crime. We believe that our parents should have known better not to do this to us, so they don't deserve our forgiveness.

**You are the main beneficiary
of your forgiveness.**

Forgiving is not for someone else; it's for you. You might think that by holding on to your anger, the other party is going to be punished somehow. But the only person you are punishing is yourself. If someone is supposed to feel guilty and ashamed of their action, they will. And if they don't think they are at fault, no matter how much you hate them, they are still not going to feel apologetic.

Even though accepting other people's apologies often helps relieve them of their pain, forgiving is mostly about giving ourselves peace of mind. Holding on to your grudges is the same as holding onto suffering. It doesn't undo your parents' wrong actions, yet it keeps your childhood pain intact. It traps you in your past and prevents you from living in the present. It is super tiring to resent someone.

Forgiveness also doesn't mean that you allow the other person to hurt you repeatedly or that you agree with their behavior. You can stay away from a person and not resent them. Forgiveness is more about letting go of your past, blame, and hurt feelings.

**Behind your hurt feelings,
there is love for your parents.**

The reason you feel so hurt by your parents is that deep down inside, you love them so much. Ever since you were a child, you have wanted their approval and love in the way you wanted it, but they didn't give it. If you did not care about your parents, you would not have felt so bothered by their actions. You feel angry toward them because you have always felt they abused and betrayed you, and taken your love for granted. So you end up distancing yourself from your parents and withholding your love.

To most people, to forgive means to stop feeling angry or resentful toward someone. It means to pardon someone for their mistakes and what they did to you. However, forgiving is also a form of giving. When you forgive, you open your heart once again and you are able to love your parents without reservation. It doesn't require us to do anything more except to go back to the natural, loving being that we all are.

Why withhold our love from our parents, or anyone else, waiting to hear these three words: *I am sorry*?

How to Forgive Your Parents?

Your parents can choose not to reflect on their past actions, but that doesn't mean you shouldn't. Forgiving is a choice. You can't help them choose, but you can make a choice yourself and not let your hurt feelings run your life anymore.

The following suggestions also apply to your inner parent. You might have followed in your parents' footsteps and done things that forsake your inner child. Here are some suggestions about how to forgive your parents, and also your inner parent.

1. Welcome your feelings.

When you try to forgive your parents, your inner child might bring out more rage and resentment. This might feel unpleasant, at first. Your mind might be filled with angry thoughts such as: *Why do I have to forgive them? They are the ones who caused me to suffer. As adults and parents, they should have known better.* If you feel this way, remind yourself that the forgiving is for your sake, not for your parents.

Instead of resisting these emotions, welcome them. Let them be. There's no need to react or express your rage. But at the same time, don't suppress your anger. Remember these emotions are layers of protection that your inner parent has put in place to protect you from your underlying pain. They need to be processed before you can delve deeper and understand your hurt feelings better.

Soothe your anger by being present with it and using empathy. You can say something like this to your inner child: *I'm here for you. I know you are angry. Let me know your pain. Share it with me. I'm here to listen.* You can also assure your inner parent that you can cope with the hurt feelings and it's okay for your inner child to express their pain. This will help your inner parent ease off its grip and let the feelings arise naturally.

When hurt feelings arise in you, just welcome them and let them be there.

Observe the hurt. Feel your bodily sensations. Talk directly to the part of your body that is feeling hurt or has the strongest reaction. This is where the inner child stores emotional pain. Ask your inner child:

- *Why do you feel this way?*
- *What causes you to feel this way?*
- *What are you afraid of?*
- *What can I do for you?*

- *How can I help you feel more at peace?*

Finally, invite your inner child to let go of the hurt feelings. If it can't, it's okay. There's no need to force or rush it. You might need to do this several times. Let your inner child let go of the pain little by little. Whenever you feel the hurt, be patient. It just means there is more inner work to be done and more emotions to be let go of. Forgiveness will come eventually, with time, but you need to have compassion for yourself first.

2. Understand your parents' intention.

A long time ago, I was curious about whether my dad had the ability to be encouraging. He often points out our mistakes, discredits our successes, and can be rather critical at times. But I had never heard my dad praise and validate me, or anyone else for that matter. So one day, I asked my dad to say three positive things about me.

"You are… very obedient," my dad replied hesitantly. I thought to myself: *Well, that's not something I would consider positive, but okay I will take it.*

"So what's the second positive thing about me?" I said. He took a while before he replied, "Obedient?"

"Isn't that the first positive thing you said about me?" I

laughed and so did the rest of the family. Then I let him off the hook because he looked so uncomfortable. But I was still curious as to why he finds it hard to praise his children, so I asked him.

"I don't want you all to get a big head," he said. In other words, he didn't want us to be arrogant and conceited.

I smiled. For the first time, I understood why my dad did what he did, and it wasn't because I was not good enough for him or that he didn't love me.

Your parents might have had good intentions at heart, but they totally messed up in the follow through.

We love to rationalize other people's actions in our own mind. *My parents criticize me because they don't love me. My parents will only love me if I am successful. My parents care about themselves and their work more than me.* But how often do we ask our parents why they behave the way they do?

Most of us *guess* our parents' intention and assume it is the truth without clarifying it with them. Instead of asking them why they do what they do, we judge, we blame, and we misunderstand based on our perception of the situation. Seldom, are we open enough to listen and give our parents the chance to share their point of view. We think we know their intentions better than they do.

I'm not saying that your parents' actions are always for the best. Sometimes, they mess it up big time. Like my dad—it never occurred to him that by not giving his children praise and approval that it would make us feel unworthy and unloved. He assumed that if he complimented us, it would make us feel overly proud of our success and we would not continue to work as hard. Instead of making me more successful, however, I had no motivation to succeed because I grew up thinking: *Why do I have to work so hard? It doesn't matter anyway. No one is going to acknowledge my success.*

Only your parents can help you fully understand their intentions. But if they are not around anymore, or if you are on bad terms with them and it's hard to talk with them, the next best alternative would be to talk to your siblings and relatives. Even though their perceptions might also be skewed, at least you will be able to get another perspective rather than be fixated on your own. No matter what the event, you and your siblings might have interpreted it very differently.

3. Do the unthinkable — empathize.

Empathizing with another person means that you are able to see yourself in their situation. If you were born in the same era and environment, and given the same knowledge as your parents, you might have made the same mistakes.

We have all done something "wrong" in our life that we regret. No matter how loving your parents are, they can't be perfect — no one can. If we were more conscious and had known better, we probably wouldn't have done some of the things we did in the past. Instead of labeling your parents as bad, controlling, or manipulative, realize that they are just unconscious. Most people are not aware that they are motivated by fear. Nor do they realize the impact of their childhood and past experiences.

We can't blame others for being unconscious. They did the best they could.

I have some students who can't answer mathematics questions, no matter how hard they try. Their parents assume they are lazy or not putting in enough effort. But the truth is you can't blame them for not doing the questions because they can't understand what they cannot see. Without someone to open them up to other perspectives, they will keep getting stuck and not know how to restart their efforts. Some students are just naturally gifted in the subject of mathematics. They are able to think in different perspectives and spot the patterns immediately, while others are gifted in other areas. It's unfair to punish someone for not trying hard enough when he or she lacks awareness and perception. It's also a waste of energy.

You can continue to resent your parents. But for all you know, your parents might not even realize what they did wrong. If they had the awareness and understood your point of view fully, they might have chosen a different path of action. They are not able to see your viewpoint because they are so fixated on their own. They thought that, as your parents, they knew better than you. It's a habit they developed when you were young and dependent on them.

However, the truth is the number of years in which our parents are parents is the same as the age of their first-born child. They spend the same amount of time learning to be parents as we spend learning about life. Can you see that when they first became parents, they really knew nothing much about parenting? Some of them didn't even know themselves well enough or how to love themselves, let alone love a child. Even though most parents do the best they can to nurture their kids, it doesn't mean they know what to do or how to do it.

As their child, can you forgive and be patient with them? Parenting is an ongoing, lifelong learning process. It's impossible to be a perfect parent. There is so much to be learned, and there are still a lot of things your parents don't know or are still learning. It might seem that the parents' job is to teach their children. However, the contrary is also true — children are here to teach their parents. Your parents each have an inner child that is hurting, but they might not realize it. The mistakes that your parents made are opportunities for them to grow and challenge their belief system. But for that to happen, you will have to give them a chance to change.

4. Live in the present.

It's hard to forgive because our mind loves to go back to the past and replay the unhappy moments. Our ego wants to make everything personal, and it keeps activating the hurt feelings we have stored in our body. If you are mindful, you will be able to bring these hurt feelings up in the present moment as they arise and release them. However, if you are not, you will end up reminding yourself how hurtful your parents were and hold on to the hatred. The former tries to resolve the hurt feelings *currently* stored in your body, while the latter brings you back to the *past*.

The past is the past.
What has happened has happened
and cannot be altered.

You can't change what has happened. You can't change what has been done to you, and your parents can't change their past actions, even if they want to. All we have is now, the present moment, and all we can change about the past are the hurt feelings we are still holding onto.

The inability to forgive your parents keeps you trapped in the past. Take a good look at them as they are now, not the image or judgment you created for them in the past. Your parents might have changed. They might have done a bad job in the past, but they could have also learned and grown. We should not rely on past information to determine the present or predict the future. You can only appreciate your parents for who they really are when you are living in the present.

Furthermore, you have changed, too, and some of the perceptions you had when you were young are no longer necessary. If you behave like the child you once were, you will trigger your parents to treat you in the same way they did when you were that child.

When you are able to live in the present, forgiveness comes naturally. You don't need to remind yourself of the things that your parents did in the past. You don't debate whether it's right or wrong to forgive them based on events that happened in the past. You choose to forgive and extend your love to them based on your current self, not your past self or past experiences.

Chapter 9

Accept Your Parents

"The greatest gift that you can give to others is the gift of unconditional love and acceptance."

— BRIAN TRACY

Six years after my Taiwan graduation trip, I found myself making my dad angry again when I decided to work as an animator in Malaysia for six months.

To be fair, there were two other overseas trips in between these two events that made my dad angry. The first one was my trip to the U.S. right after the Boston Marathon bombing in 2013. My dad was already unhappy that I was going to a country with no strict gun control. But to make things worse, Boston was part of my itinerary.

My second trip was to Bangkok in 2014, at the same time the Thai Army declared martial law nationwide because of a political crisis and protest. To appease my dad, I was the only person in my group of friends to withdraw from the Bangkok trip and forfeit my flight. I did go to the United States, though, because I had already paid a lot of money for the flights and accommodations.

However, my travel to Taiwan was quite different. I was going to another country to work, not for a holiday. And I would be gone for six months, not just a week! Before the animation studio accepted me, I did my art test and job interview through Skype secretly in my room. If I didn't get hired, my dad wouldn't have to know about it and I could just carry on with my life as usual.

But as you know, I was hired, and I had mixed feelings of happiness, excitement, and… apprehension. It meant that I had to break the news to my dad, and I didn't think he was going to receive it well.

"What good is that?" he said. *Ouch!* This was the first thing my dad said when he heard the news. Then he continued, "Are you crazy? There is work in Singapore and you don't do that work. Why do you want to go to Malaysia where the exchange rate is much worse than Singapore?"

My mom chimed in, "I know you don't want to be an accountant. But don't they have animation jobs in

Singapore? Why do you have to go to Malaysia?"

My dad resumed his lecture, "Usually, Malaysians come to Singapore for work. I never heard of people from Singapore going to Malaysia to find a job."

For the next hour or so, they tried to talk convince me that they knew what was best for me. I had expected this kind of response, but it still hurt that my parents were not supportive of my decision.

Never treat your parents' love for you as a nuisance, even when it is not expressed in the way you want it to be.

Days later, I was on my way to Malaysia, and both my parents and my aunt traveled with me on the bus. If I had been ten years younger, I would have felt annoyed and embarrassed to be accompanied by my parents. But now that I'm much older, I don't mind having them follow me around because it gives them peace of mind. Now I realize that it's just their way of expressing love.

Despite my dad's anger and dissatisfaction with my career path, I knew he was worried about me. In his mind, Malaysia is an unsafe place to live. It has a much higher crime rate than Singapore, so before I left he kept reminding me to be careful. He even volunteered to accompany me because he felt insecure about my traveling alone. After all, he's the lion and I'm his cub, and no one touches his cub.

Even though he can be protective, controlling, and stifling at times, I am unable to be mad at him, no matter how unsupportive he is of my career. In the end, I know he cares about me. This is the beauty of parental love, and I learn to cherish it more and more as I grow older. But it wasn't always easy. Sometimes, I felt like one of his possessions.

When I was growing up, I believed that my parents didn't love me. I thought they cared more about money and their own images than me. Partly, it was also because I was the middle child and I am overly accommodating. I was always giving in to my elder and younger brothers, and I didn't get the attention that I desired. So it made me feel a little invisible and unimportant growing up. But now I realize this misunderstanding is mostly due to the different love languages and personalities that my parents and I have.

Different Love Languages

In his book, *The Five Love Languages*, Gary Chapman explains how different people with different personalities express love in different ways. He outlines five languages of love, as follows:

- Words of affirmation
- Quality time
- Receiving gifts
- Acts of service
- Physical touch

These love languages don't just apply to romantic relationships. They also apply to the parent-child relationship.

Many years ago, I did the quiz and found out that my primary love language is quality time and my secondary love language is physical touch. As a child, I yearned for attention, emotional connection, and hugs from my parents. I wanted to spend quality time with them but they were always working and they never wanted to talk about emotions or have a deeper connection with me. Furthermore, growing up in an Asian family, parents don't usually hug their children, especially the dads.

Most importantly, I realize that my parents have love languages that I scored low in on the quiz. My dad expresses his love through action. When our computers wouldn't work, he would be there to help fix them. If we needed advice on what IT gadgets to buy or stocks to invest in, he would offer his advice. But we didn't expect him to praise us or give us a pat on your back when we did something well. This wasn't something he was comfortable with giving.

My mom, on the other hand, expresses love through giving and receiving gifts. For the longest time, I didn't understand why my mom lights up whenever she receives money and gifts. I don't experience the same joy when I receive gifts from others. Not only does she enjoy receiving gifts, she also enjoys giving things away to other people, sometimes even food intended for our family. So I used to think that she loved others more than her children. She would also buy me things that I didn't really need, and our conversations would often revolve around tangible things such as money, food, clothing, astrology, and celebrities, but nothing deeper.

Even though my parents took good care of my survival needs, I didn't feel loved growing up because that wasn't how I interpret love. I didn't know that when my dad fixes my computer or when my mom buys me something that this is their way of showing me love. As a child, I just wanted to have a deeper relationship and connection with my parents. I hoped they would take the time to listen to me and understand my feelings. When I had trouble in school, I wished they were there to talk to me and not just point out my mistakes or how I could have done better.

**Realize your parents might never love you
the way you have always wanted them to.**

Sometimes, when I talked to my parents, I couldn't help but think that they were more concerned about themselves than me. For example, when I was depressed because of my first job and told them it made me feel like killing myself, my mom's first reaction was to reprimand me: "Why are you so inconsiderate? What will happen to us if you die? We spent so much time, money, and effort to raise you up, but all you can think of is dying." My comment about suicide was a careless expression from me in the heat of the moment, and I understand how bad they must have felt to hear me say it. But what about how I feel? My emotions are also important.

I used to think that my parents didn't care about me. Instead of acknowledging my emotions, most of the time, I have to soothe *their* emotions and make sure *they* don't get angry or upset. It's hard for me to have emotional and physical intimacy with others because the closest people in my life don't want to have that kind of intimacy with me. So it's rather confusing and uncomfortable when someone I barely know tries to be my best buddy and puts his or her arms around me.

Now that I understand that my parents have a different way of expressing love, I don't expect them to love me the way I've always wanted them to love me. Instead, whenever I notice they are expressing love in their language, I remind myself to appreciate it and not take their love for granted. I have learned to accept my parents for who they are.

How to Accept Your Parents for Who They Are

Conflicts are bound to arise when you have a different love language and personality from your parents. However, to let go of your childhood grief and heal your inner child, it's important to accept your parents for who they are. If not, your resistance toward them is going to keep you trapped in anger and resentment.

If forgiving your parents is about healing your past, then accepting them is about healing your relationship with them in the present.

Here are three suggestions for how you can learn to accept your parents:

1. Understand what they can give and cannot give.

All children deserve loving, kind, and supportive parents, but not everyone gets them. Some parents just can't be warm, caring, and nurturing even though they love you. It's not part of their habits and personality. Others have their own issues that they can't resolve and are wrapped up in their own problems. If they can't even provide love to themselves, how can they give you the love you need?

Once you realize and accept that what your parents can give you doesn't align with what you need, you will stop seeking approval and love from them.

Why keep knocking at the same door that doesn't open?

Asking someone who isn't comfortable with giving praise to praise you sets you up for disappointment. You already know they won't give you the approval you want.

I know that my dad has a supervisory instinct and he doesn't want us to get conceited, so he would never affirm or praise us. Rather than seeking approval from him or showing him how successful I am, nowadays I only go to him when I need help. This allows him to express his love toward me using actions instead of words. Also, realizing that my parents are not the kind of people who feel comfortable talking about emotions, I stopped expecting them to have deep conversations with me. Instead, I talk to my younger brother, who is more comfortable with sharing deeper thoughts and feelings, and I also have more like-minded friends who are willing to connect with me at this level.

One reason why we find it difficult to accept someone like our parents is that we expect them to do what we want:

- My parents should have acknowledged my effort.
- My parents should have been more supportive of my choices.
- They shouldn't have given birth to me if they don't care about me.
- He should have known better not to do this.
- She should have remembered my birthday.

The truth is we have too high an expectation for others. We can't expect others to be just like us. They are not us. They don't have the same desires and preferences as us. Instead of demanding love and attention from your parents, position yourself in such a way that you can receive their unique expression of love.

2. Change your perspective from getting to learning.

We are born into a family for a reason: growth. Most of us don't have parents who share the same personalities and preferences as we do. We need to learn how to get along with our family members. This learning process not only helps us grow, it helps our parents grow, too.

Once an ex-colleague asked me, "How can I teach my daughter mathematics? I get so impatient when she doesn't understand simple additions and subtractions." This ex-colleague fails to see that perhaps it's not about teaching her daughter mathematics. It's about learning to be more patient with her daughter.

Like in my case, I was meant to challenge my dad's insecurities, fears, and beliefs. My purpose was to encourage him to be more open-minded, trusting, and accepting. He was meant to test and develop my resilience and persistence in pursuing my dreams. We are fated to push each other's emotional "buttons" and learn how to overcome our negativity.

Your parents can help you become a better person, no matter what they did or did not do.

If you get this, it will be so much easier to accept your parents and their actions. The worst thing you can do is to compare them with other parents. Don't ask why other people have parents who are nurturing and supportive, but you have parents who are abusive, unreasonable, and difficult to deal with. A comparison like this will just make you feel envious and like a victim. Everyone's lesson is different. If this is the lesson that has been given to you, it means that this is the area you need growth in, so make the best of it.

Your parents can also be your spiritual teachers. If you treat them as individuals who are here to teach something valuable, your relationship with them will naturally improve. However, if you treat them like enemies or someone to get love from, then you will continue to suffer.

3. Process your grief instead of trying to change your parents.

It's very tempting for us to try to "fix" our parents, especially if we have a tendency to help others. But from experience, I can say it rarely works. We only make things worse when we try to change someone else. Furthermore, when we try to fix our parents, isn't it the same as them trying to change us — as though there is something wrong with us? Both are the product of non-acceptance.

Yes, your parents might have some issues of their own that they need to resolve. And yes, we help each other grow in a family. But ultimately, whether a person decides to change or not depends solely on the person. They choose whether to self-reflect and grow or remain as they are. Only they can help themselves. It's not up to you to decide.

To accept your parents, allow them to grow on their own terms and at their own pace. People only change when they choose to change. The more you tell someone to do something, the more they don't want to do it. Instead, let your parents choose their own path and accept the fact that they might never change. You might be the only person who wants them to change, but they don't want to, even though you think it's good for them.

Stop having the fantasy that one day your parents will be different than they are.

When we cannot accept another person, it's never about the other person. It's always about us. We are trying to control other people's actions and behaviors because we don't want to be in touch with our own grief. Accepting our parents for who they are means we have to face reality and give up our fantasies. It means we have to come to terms with the fact that they are not as supportive and nurturing as we imagine or desire them to be. It also means we have to accept that we can't get our parents to love us the way we want them to love us, and we are powerless in getting love from our parents, or anyone else for that matter. The fantasy we have about our parents only covers up the sorrow we experienced as children. Realizing it's just a fantasy will only bring back our childhood grief.

However, we can only be finally free by processing our different emotions — anger, resentment, shame, fear, and grief — and accepting our parents for who they are. Only through our acceptance of our parents can we embrace the responsibility to love ourselves and not wait or depend on them to take care of our needs. The only way to improve our relationships with our parents is to change the way we relate to them. For this, we must also change.

Being Your Own Parent

"A baby is born with a need to be loved - and never outgrows it."

— FRANK A. CLARK

Three months after I left my part-time work in my ex-company, I was asked to help out again. This time, another one of my friends needed to have some minor surgery on her eyelid. It felt like a test to see if I had learned anything from my previous experience.

What was different this second time was that I consulted my inner child first. I made sure I understood how the child felt about going back to work before I agreed to the job. Because I had established a mutual understanding between my inner child and inner parent, I was in complete bliss working as an accountant for the one month. Ever since, my inner child has been very open in sharing how it feels, either through thoughts, emotions, or bodily sensations. My inner parent has also been empathetic and patient with my inner child. There is a good rapport between the two. Even if there is an inner conflict, I am aware of it, which is better than having the inner child sabotage my efforts at the subconscious level.

The path to self-compassion is easy when you are on your own and not triggered by anyone else or external events. However, we know this is not practical. We can't avoid certain people or events. There will always be people who are like your parents and events that will challenge your ability to love yourself. There might be people who criticize and disapprove of you. You might feel rejected by other people's actions or inactions. At moments like these, you need to know how to calm yourself down and undo the hurt that gets triggered in your inner child. In fact, every time the pain comes up, it's an opportunity to practice self-love. It's an opportunity to further let go of the pain and fear your inner child carries.

Learning how to reconcile the inner parent and inner child within you will help you in your relationships with others. You understand what you need, and rather than finding others like your parents and spouse and expecting them to know and provide what you need, you fulfill your own needs. This relieves your partners and friends of the stress of having to meet your expectations, and there will also be less chance of you feeling disappointed when they don't do what you expect them to do. Of course, this doesn't mean that we don't need support from others while we do our inner work. It's beautiful to find someone who can love you the same way you love yourself and have a relationship with him or her. But this is just an added bonus.

The most important relationship will always be the relationship you have with yourself.

When you realize that *you are love*, there is no need to seek love from someone else. You just need to remind yourself to tap into the love that is always within you and supporting you.

Also, when you become a parent, you will know how to take care of your child because you have practiced loving yourself first. You know how powerless a child feels and you will be able to love him or her in a way that is both protective and nurturing. You will also know not to let your parental ego get in the way of connecting with your child. Most importantly, you can stop the cycle and not pass on the pain your inner child has experienced to your own child.

Many of us choose to blame our parents for our upbringing. We feel frustrated that they don't reflect and improve themselves. But by doing so, we also pass down resentment and anger to our future generations. Remember, behind the anger, there is hurt. Behind the hurt, there is love. When you dig deep enough, you will be able to find love for your parents.

No matter what happened in the past, you can love yourself the way you wanted your parents to love you. You are an adult now. Be your own parent.

Did You Like *Parent Yourself Again*?

Thank you for purchasing my book and spending the time to read it.

Before you go, I'd like to ask you for a small favor. Could you please take a couple of minutes to leave a review for this book on Amazon?

Your feedback will not only help me grow as an author; it will also help those readers who need to hear the message in this book. So, thank you!

Please leave a review at:

http://www.nerdycreator.com/parent-yourself-again.

Recommended Reading

Self-Therapy: A Step-By-Step Guide to Creating Wholeness and Healing Your Inner Child Using IFS, A New, Cutting-Edge Psychotherapy by Jay Earley; 2009; Pattern System Books, Larkspur, California.

The Body Keeps the Score: Brain, Mind, and Body in the Healing of Trauma by Bessel van der Kolk; 2015; Penguin Books, New York, New York.

Waking the Tiger: Healing Trauma by Peter A. Levine and Ann Frederick; 1997; North Atlantic Books, Berkeley, California.

Reconciliation: Healing the Inner Child by Thich Nhat Hanh; 2010; Parallax Press, Berkeley, California.

To read more books on self-compassion and mindfulness, visit this URL: http://www.nerdycreator.com/bookclub/

Here are more books by Yong Kang:

The Disbelief Habit: How to Use Doubt to Make Peace with Your Inner Critic (Self-Compassion Book 2)

Empty Your Cup: Why We Have Low Self-Esteem and How Mindfulness Can Help (Self-Compassion Book 1)

The Emotional Gift: Memoir of a Highly Sensitive Person Who Overcame Depression

Fearless Passion: Find the Courage to Do What You Love

To see the latest books by the author, please go to www.nerdycreator.com/books.

About the Author

Yong Kang Chan, best known as Nerdy Creator, is a blogger, mindfulness teacher, and private tutor. Having low self-esteem growing up, he has read a lot of books on personal growth, psychology, and spirituality.

Based in Singapore, Yong Kang teaches mathematics and accounting to his students. On his website, he writes blog posts on self-compassion and mindfulness to help introverts and people with low self-esteem.

Please visit his website at www.nerdycreator.com.

Printed in Great
Britain
by Amazon